# Knitted Sweaters for Every Season

# Nancie M. Wiseman

# Knitted Sweaters

# *for Every Season*

## 4 Techniques, 16 Sweaters, and More!

*Martingale*™
& COMPANY

## DEDICATION

To THAYES and Arthur Wiseman, my parents. My mother taught me sewing, knitting, crochet, and the patience to do them all. My father, who passed away when I was young, taught me to be strong as well as self-sufficient. May you both rest in peace.

◆  ◆  ◆

## ACKNOWLEDGMENTS

THANK YOU to my husband, Bill Attwater, who does the cooking, the errand running, and brings me lattes from town while I work at the computer. You are truly a treasure I hold dear.

Thank you to all the yarn companies listed in the back of the book for your willingness to send yarn for the projects in this book. Without you, these garments would have remained designs in my head instead of actual sweaters with directions. Those of us who knit applaud you and your yarns.

Also a big thank you to Martingale & Company for producing the most beautiful knitting books—ever. Thank you for turning my vision and knitting into this wonderful book.

And to Ursula Reikes (aka Ricky). Your talent, wisdom, and love of knitting make it a joy to work with you. I feel like I have gained a friend and an editor I hold dear. Thank you so much for all of your help.—Nancie (aka Lucy)

## CREDITS

| | |
|---|---|
| President | Nancy J. Martin |
| CEO | Daniel J. Martin |
| Publisher | Jane Hamada |
| Editorial Director | Mary V. Green |
| Managing Editor | Tina Cook |
| Technical Editor | Ursula Reikes |
| Copy Editor | Karen Koll |
| Design Director | Stan Green |
| Illustrators | Robin Strobel, Laurel Strand |
| Cover and Text Designer | Trina Stahl |
| Fashion Photographer | Anna Midori Abe |
| Studio Photographer | Brent Kane |

*Martingale*™
& COMPANY

Knitted Sweaters for Every Season: 4 Techniques, 16 Sweaters, and More!
© 2002 by Nancie M. Wiseman

Martingale & Company
20205 144th Avenue NE
Woodinville, WA 98072-8478 USA
www.martingale-pub.com

Printed in Singapore
07 06 05 04 03 02   8 7 6 5 4 3 2 1

## MISSION STATEMENT

*We are dedicated to providing quality products and service by working together to inspire creativity and to enrich the lives we touch.*

**Library of Congress Cataloging-in-Publication Data is available upon request.**

**ISBN 1-56477-401-5**

# Contents

# Preface

THE FOUR SEASONS: what do they represent to you?

**Spring:** renewal, flowers in bloom, melting snow, Easter, Mother's Day, weddings.

**Summer:** lazy days, warm weather, boating, the beach, summer camp, vacations.

**Fall:** my favorite season. Warm colors, back to school, crisp afternoons, the smell of apples and cinnamon.

**Winter:** Sparkling white lights, the holidays, snow, rain, skiing, the warmth of a fire, a new year.

The seasons influence the way we live, dress, and work. Our knitting is seasonal too. In theory, we should start a spring garment in winter to be able to wear it in the spring. This can be a problem if the patterns for spring aren't out in the winter. In this book, however, you'll find sweaters for every season, so you can knit no matter what time of year it is or what the weather is like where you live. You'll have to agree that if you're a die-hard knitter, it doesn't matter what the weather is—it's always sweater weather.

# Introduction

WHEN I FINISHED *Knitted Shawls, Stoles, and Scarves* (Martingale & Company, 2001), I desperately wanted to use some of the techniques from that book in sweaters. I chose four of my favorite techniques and began working them into vests, sweaters, and coats. Those four techniques, which are listed below and featured in this book, result in some of the most intriguing design elements used in knitting today.

♦ Slipped stitches and mosaic stitches
♦ Interlocking squares and diamonds
♦ Diagonal knitting
♦ Short rows and short-rows color work

Early on, I realized that I needed to make sure the techniques would work in different weights and styles of yarn, so I knitted sweaters for each season of the year. As a result, no matter where you live, what the season is, or what the climate is like, you can start a sweater that is perfect for you. Each technique in the book includes comprehensive how-to information, a pattern for a simple purse that is small and easy to complete so you can learn the basics before you move on to garments, and directions for four garments—one for every season.

Now you have to decide which technique you want to learn and which project you want to knit first. I hope you enjoy each of the techniques and designs as much as I enjoyed creating and knitting them.

# Techniques

## CASTING ON

### Cable Cast On

Use cable cast on when there is already knitting on the needles. You can use it to start a project as well, but it tends to be a little tight unless you take care to make it loose. This cast on is used extensively in the "Diagonal Knitting" and "Short Rows" sections of the book.

To work this cast on, hold the needle with the stitches on it in your left hand. *Knit a stitch by inserting the right needle between the first 2 stitches on the left needle. Place the new stitch on the left needle by inserting the left needle into the new stitch from the right side, or the side by your right thumb.* Repeat from * to * for as many stitches as required.

### Provisional Cast On

Using contrasting cotton yarn and a size G or H hook, crochet a loose chain with the number of stitches needed for the cast on of the sweater, plus 4 or 5 extra. Finish off, cut yarn, and tie a knot in the tail you ended with. The knot will tell you from what end to pull out the chain. You will remove this chain later, so it is good to use cotton yarn, because it doesn't leave little bits of fiber behind when it is removed.

Turn the chain to the wrong side. Using the sweater yarn and the appropriate-sized needle, pick up a stitch into the loop on the wrong side of the chain. Pick up as many stitches as required; you may skip stitches on the chain if it gets too tight or if you can't see where to pick up the stitches. Proceed with sweater directions until directed to remove the chain.

To remove the chain, gently "unzip" the chain from the end with the knot on the tail (this is the only end from which the chain will "unzip"). At the same time, place the stitches in the sweater yarn on the knitting needle 1 stitch at a time. You can use a needle 1 to 2 sizes smaller than the needle used to pick up the stitches. Be careful that you don't drop stitches by pulling out too much of the chain at one time.

## JOINING SEAMS

### Knitting Together Hem and Body Stitches

When directed to knit together the hem and body stitches with provisional cast on, as in the Hemmed Coat with Diagonal Collar and Cuffs, page 68, work as follows. Remove the crochet chain from the cast on and place the cast-on stitches on a smaller needle as directed in "Provisional Cast On" (1) With wrong sides of the hem and body together, hold the needle with the body stitches in the left hand and fold the hem stitches up and to the back of the work. With a third needle, knit together 1

stitch from the body needle and 1 stitch from the hem needle across the row (2). You will be 1 stitch short on the hem needle. Knit the last stitch on the body needle by itself (with no accompanying hem stitch). Proceed with pattern, using the appropriate needle specified for the rest of the garment.

### Grafting (also called Kitchener Stitch)

To join seams invisibly, use grafting. Grafting is quite commonly used to join the toe of a sock, but it is very useful for other seams as well. There are many pictures of this technique in knitting books, but it is difficult to see how the yarn and stitches are worked, because the pictures show the new stitch being made with the existing stitches off the needle. In reality that can't be done, because the knitting would begin to unravel.

My method for this technique is a bit more foolproof and removes a lot of frustration if you lose your place. Using contrasting yarn (I use cotton because it doesn't leave little bits of fiber behind), work about 4 rows of stockinette stitch on each edge that is to be joined. Bind off. Gently press and steam only the contrasting stitches so they are very flat and very stable. *Do not* steam the rest of the knitting. Thread a blunt tapestry needle with the sweater yarn; you can use tails left from your knitting if they are long enough to do a whole row. Fold the contrasting sections out of the way and hold the 2 sections with the right side facing up. Follow the path of the waste yarn to create a row of knitting to join the 2 pieces together. Start by going under the first loop of the knit stitch on the back piece, then through the first loop on the front piece. For the rest of the row, go under 2 loops of the stitch alternating from the back (1) to the front piece (2), adjusting the tension as you go to match the tension of the knitting. Remove the waste yarn.

# BINDING OFF

## Three-Stitch I-Cord Bind Off (3-St I-cord BO)

Three-stitch I-cord bind off is used when there are existing stitches on a needle. It is a way of binding off the stitches and leaving a rounded edge. With the existing stitches on the left needle, cast on 3 stitches to the same needle in cable cast on (1). *Knit 2 stitches. Slip, slip, knit with third cast-on stitch and 1 stitch from the existing stitches (2). Slip 3 stitches on right needle back to left needle.* Repeat from * to * around. Finish off.

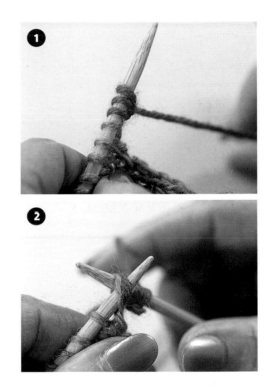

## Two-Stitch I-Cord Bind Off (2-St I-cord BO)

Work two-stitch I-cord bind off the same as three-stitch I-cord bind off, but cast on 2 stitches instead of 3.

## Attached I Cord

Use attached I cord when there are no stitches on the needle to join the I cord to. Using double-pointed needles, cast on 3 stitches. Do not turn. *Knit 2 stitches, pulling yarn tightly across the back to make a tube, slip the third stitch, pick up a stitch (1) into the border you are attaching the I cord to, knit 2 stitches together (2). Do not turn. Slide the stitches to the opposite end of the needle and repeat from *, picking up stitches as designated in pattern.

## Three-Needle Bind Off (3-Needle BO)

Place stitches to be joined on needles, with needle points toward the right, and the right sides of the knitting together. *Knit together 1 stitch from the front needle and 1 stitch from the back needle* (1), (2). Repeat from * to *. When there are 2 stitches on the right needle, bind off loosely (3). Repeat from * to * across. Finish off last stitch.

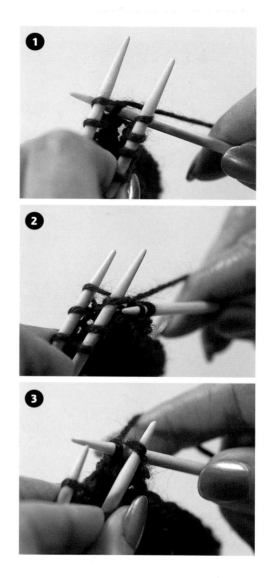

# OTHER KNITTING BASICS

## I Cord

Using double-pointed needles, cast on 2 to 5 stitches and knit across. *Do not turn. Slide the stitches to the opposite end of the needle. Knit across the row, pulling the working yarn tightly across the back of the work, forming a tube.* Continue from * to * for desired length. Bind off.

## Pick Up and Knit (PU)

When directed to pick up a stitch, insert the right needle into existing knitting, wrap the yarn around the right needle tip, and knit the new stitch onto the needle. Always pick up and knit with right side facing unless instructed otherwise.

## Place Marker (PM)

Place a ring marker on the right needle between stitches as directed in pattern. When you come to the marker on subsequent rows, slip it from the left needle to the right needle. It is there to help you know when to perform a specific action.

## Knitting In Ends

Knitting in ends is a technique used extensively in the "Interlocking Squares and Diamonds" projects. To change colors when picking up new stitches or working with existing stitches, knit the first stitch in the new color. Hold the tail of the new yarn and the tail of the old yarn in your left hand above the needles and to the wrong side (1). *Insert the right needle into the next stitch, hold the tails under the right needle tip (2), and knit the next stitch. Do not knit the tails into the stitch. Insert the right needle into the next stitch, hold the tails above, and knit the stitch (3).* Repeat from * to * for about 5 to 8 stitches. This process weaves in the tails on the wrong side as you knit, eliminating the need to weave them in later.

## Decreasing

### Slip, Slip, Knit (SSK)

Slip 1 stitch from the left needle to the right needle as if to knit. Slip the next stitch on the left needle as if to knit. With the stitches on the right needle, insert the left needle from left to right through the front of the stitches. Wrap the yarn around the right needle and knit the 2 stitches together.

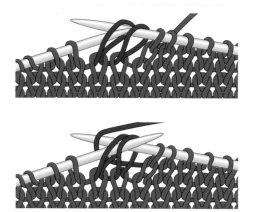

### Slip, Slip, Slip, Knit (SSSK)

Worked the same as slip, slip, knit, except with 3 stitches instead of 2.

### Central Chain Decrease (CCD)

Slip the next 2 stitches together as if to knit. Knit 1; pass the 2 slipped stitches over.

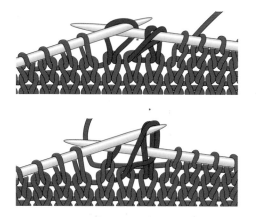

### Slip, Slip, Purl (SSP)

Slip the first stitch on the left needle to the right needle as if to knit. Slip another stitch to the right needle as if to knit. Insert the left knitting needle into the front of the 2 stitches and transfer them back to the left needle. Insert the right needle tip into the back of the 2 stitches from left to right. Purl the 2 stitches together.

## CROCHETED EDGES

### Single Crochet

With right side of work facing and starting at right edge of the knitting, insert the crochet hook into the knitting, yarn over the hook, bring the new stitch through the knitting. *Insert the hook into the next stitch, yarn over the hook, bring the new stitch through the knitting. Yarn over the hook and draw through 2 loops on hook.* Repeat from * to *, finish off when edging is completed. Do not finish off if a row of reverse single crochet is to follow.

## Reverse Single Crochet (or Crab Stitch)

With right side of work facing, chain one, *insert the crochet hook into the first single crochet (or knit stitch) to the right, yarn over the hook, bring the new stitch through to the right side. Yarn over the hook and pull yarn through both loops on needle.* Repeat from * to * until all stitches are used, finish off. This stitch will be a bit awkward to work; it should leave a twisted stitch at the top of the work.

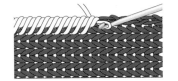

Reverse single crochet shown on knit edge

# Abbreviations

| | | | | |
|---|---|---|---|---|
| **approx** | approximately | | **PM** | place marker |
| **beg** | begin(ning) | | **psso** | pass slipped stitch(es) over |
| **BO** | bind off | | **P2tog** | purl 2 together |
| **CC** | contrasting color | | **PU** | pick up and knit |
| **CCD** | central chain decrease | | **pw** | purlwise |
| **ch** | chain | | **rem** | remaining |
| **circ** | circular | | **rep** | repeat |
| **cn** | cable needle | | **RS** | right side |
| **CO** | cast on | | **RSR** | right side row |
| **cont** | continue | | **sc** | single crochet |
| **dec** | decrease | | **sl st** | slip stitch |
| **dpn** | double-pointed needle | | **SSK** | slip, slip, knit |
| **EOR** | every other row | | **SSSK** | slip, slip, slip, knit |
| **g** | gram | | **SSP** | slip, slip, purl |
| **inc** | increase | | **st(s)** | stitch(es) |
| **K** | knit | | **St st** | stockinette stitch |
| **K2tog** | knit 2 together | | **tog** | together |
| **K2tog tbl** | knit 2 together through the back loop | | **W and T** | wrap and turn |
| **kw** | knitwise | | **wyib** | with yarn in back |
| **M1** | make 1 stitch | | **wyif** | with yarn in front |
| **MC** | main color | | **WS** | wrong side |
| **oz** | ounces | | **WSR** | wrong side row |
| **P** | purl | | **yds** | yards |
| **patt** | pattern | | **YO** | yarn over |

# *Slipped Stitches*

SLIPPED AND MOSAIC STITCHES offer so much variety, it is hard to choose which pattern to knit. Either can easily turn a plain sweater into a dramatic garment with color and texture. There is a slight difference between slipped stitches and mosaic stitches, but the difference can dramatically change the look of the garment.

- Slipped-stitch patterns are usually worked in stockinette stitch, slipping the same stitch on both the wrong and right side.

- In mosaic-stitch patterns, the stitch that was knit on the right side is also knit on the wrong side, and the same stitch that was slipped on the right side gets slipped on the wrong side.

# and Mosaic Stitches

## INCREASING AND DECREASING IN PATTERN STITCHES

There is one small problem when working with most pattern stitches, including slipped and mosaic stitches, and that is maintaining the pattern when you have to increase or decrease. Let's use a simple pattern to demonstrate how to work increases into a pattern stitch.

**Pattern Stitch**

K 2 setup rows in MC.

Rows 1 and 3 in CC1: (K4, sl 1) to end, K4.

Rows 2 and 4 in CC2: (P4, sl 1) to end, P4.

Rows 5 and 6: K across in MC.

Rep rows 1–6.

If the pattern requires you to increase 1 stitch at each end on row 6, there will be an extra stitch at both ends for the next repeat of the pattern. To keep the slipped stitches in the right place as you increase, you need to increase the number of stitches before and after the pattern repeat, which is shown in parentheses. The pattern repeat in this example ends with sl 1. Incorporate the increases into the rows as follows:

Rows 1 and 3: sl 1, (K4, sl 1) to end, K4, sl 1.

Rows 2 and 4: sl 1, (P4, sl 1) to end, P4, sl 1.

Row 5: Knit.

Row 6: Knit across, inc 1 st at beg and end of row.

Next repeat:

Rows 1 and 3: K1, sl 1, (K4, sl 1) to end, K4, sl 1, K1.

Rows 2 and 4: P1, sl 1, (P4, sl 1) to end, P4, sl 1, P1.

Row 5: Knit.

Row 6: Knit across, inc 1 st at beg and end of row.

Next repeat:

Rows 1 and 3: K2, sl 1, (K4, sl 1) to end, K4, sl 1, K2.

Rows 2 and 4: P2, sl 1, (P4, sl 1) to end, P4, sl 1, P2.

Row 5: Knit.

Row 6: Knit across, inc 1 st at beg and end of row.

Next repeat:

Rows 1 and 3: K3, sl 1, (K4, sl 1) to end, K4, sl 1, K3.

Rows 2 and 4: P3, sl 1, (P4, sl 1) to end, P4, sl 1, P3.

Row 5: Knit.

Adding 2 more increases on row 6 brings you back to the original repeat of the pattern, plus 2 extra repeats, 1 at each end.

Rows 1 and 3: (K4, sl 1) to end, K4.

Rows 2 and 4: (P4, sl 1) to end, P4.

Rows 5 and 6: Knit.

Work decreases into a pattern by reducing the number of stitches before and after the pattern repeat, and fitting the pattern in to accommodate the loss of sts.

---
## TIP
---

Learn to "read" your knitting by learning to recognize what happens when you perform a certain action. This will help you maintain the pattern stitch much more easily. For example, when you slip 1 stitch, look and see what happens to that stitch in subsequent rows. You will get better at this the more you practice it. Don't knit "blindly." Look at your knitting after every few rows; this will help you spot mistakes sooner and save you a lot of ripping out.

# Summer Slip-Stitch Tote Bag

## KNITTED MEASUREMENTS

16" wide x 15" high x 3" deep

## MATERIALS

- Newport Cotton by Classic Elite Yarns (100% mercerized cotton, 70yds/50g)
  - 6 skeins color 2088 (MC)
  - 1 skein color 2036 (CC1)
  - 1 skein color 2068 (CC2)
- Sizes 7 and 8 straight needles, or size required to obtain gauge
- 2 size 6 double-pointed needles
- 1 yd. fabric for lining
- 2 yds. Pellon Craft-Fuse
- 1 yd. Heat 'n Bond Lite Iron-on Adhesive
- 1 yd. Pellon Thermolam (needle-punched polyester fleece)
- 7" zipper for pocket
- 4 buttons, 1" diameter

## GAUGE

18 sts and 22 rows = 4" in stockinette stitch on size 8 needles

## BOTTOM

WITH SIZE 8 needles and MC, CO 10 sts, work 2 rows in St st. Cont in St st, inc 1 st at beg and end of EOR 5 times—20 sts. Cont in St st for 9" from last inc. Dec 1 st at beg and end of EOR 5 times. BO all sts. Trace the shape of the bottom on a piece of paper to use for lining pattern later.

## POCKETS

**MARK CENTER of each long side of bottom. With RS facing, count 16 rows from the right. Starting at this point, PU 33 sts with MC. There should be 16 rows to the left of the pocket remaining. P back, beg sl st pattern as follows. Do not cut yarns; carry loosely up the edge.

- **Row 1 (RS):** With CC1, K1, *K3, sl 1 wyib*; rep from * to *, end K4.
- **Row 2:** With CC1, K1, *K3, sl 1 wyif*; rep from * to *, end K4.
- **Row 3:** With MC, K2, *sl 1 wyib, K3*; rep from * to *, end sl 1, K2.
- **Row 4:** With MC, P2, *sl 1, wyif, P3*; rep from * to *, end sl 1, P2.
- **Rows 5 and 6:** With CC2, rep rows 1 and 2.
- **Rows 7 and 8:** With MC, rep rows 3 and 4.

Rep rows 1 through 8 for 7", ending with MC. K 4 rows, work 2-st I-cord BO (see page 10), finish off. Rep from ** for other side. Trace the pocket shape on a piece of paper to use for lining pattern later.

## BODY

WITH RS of bottom of bag facing, use size 8 needles and MC to start at center of CO edge and PU 59 sts across one side of bottom with pocket folded toward you. Work in St st, inc 1 st at each end on row 5 and then every 6 rows 10 times. Cont in St st until body measures 14" from picked-up edge. Change to size 7 needles, K 2 rows in MC, K 2 rows in CC1, K 2 rows in MC, K 2 rows in CC2, K 2 rows in MC, work 2-st I-cord BO. Finish off. Rep for other side. Trace the body shape on a piece of paper to use for lining pattern later.

## HANDLES

MAKE 2 lengths of I cord in each color. With size 6 dpn, work 3-st I-cord (see page 11) for approximately 40". BO all sts. Stretch and pin to about 45". Spray with water and allow to dry before removing.

## FINISHING

SEE "LINING PURSES" on page 124 for lining instructions. Braid 1 strand in each of 3 colors of I-cord handles together. Sew the braid firmly to the bag, starting at the bottom edge along the side of the pocket and continuing up to the top edge of the bag. Be careful not to twist. Sew to opposite side of same pocket. Repeat for other handle. Add buttons as shown in photo.

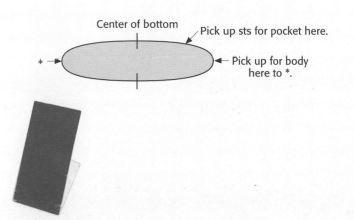

Center of bottom

Pick up sts for pocket here.

*

Pick up for body here to *.

# String of Pearls Slip-Stitch Pullover

## KNITTED MEASUREMENTS

SIZES: Small (Medium, Large)
FINISHED BUST: 37 (41, 45)"
LENGTH: 21 (22, 23½)"

## MATERIALS

◆ String of Pearls by Muench Yarns (70% cotton, 20% viscose, 10% polyester, 99yds/50g)
  · 11 (12, 14) skeins color 4003 (MC)
  · 1 (1, 1) skein color 4001 (CC)
◆ Sizes 6 and 7 straight needles, or size required to obtain gauge
◆ Size 6 circular needles (16")
◆ 2 stitch holders

## GAUGE

20 sts and 28 rows = 4" in stockinette stitch on size 7 needles.

## BACK

### Border

WITH SIZE 6 straight needles and MC, CO 92 (102, 112) sts. **Row 1 (WS):** K3, (sl 1, K4) across, end K3. **Row 2:** K across. Rep these 2 rows for 1 (1, 1¼)", ending with row 1.

### Body

CHANGE TO size 7 needles and CC, K18 (3, 8), *[(K1, YO) 3 times, K1] all in same st, making 7 sts out of 1, K 19*, rep from * to * 1 (2, 2) times, [(K1, YO) 3 times, K1] all in same st, K33 (38, 43). **Next row:** K across.

Change to MC. **Row 1:** K17 (2, 7), (K2tog, K5, SSK, K17) 2 (3, 3) times, K2tog, K5, SSK, K32 (37, 42). **Row 2:** P32 (37, 42), (SSP, P1, sl 1 wyif, P1, P2tog, P17) 2 (3, 3) times, SSP, P1, sl 1 wyif, P1, P2tog, P17 (2, 7). **Row 3:** K17 (2, 7), (K2tog, sl 1 wyib, SSK, K17) 2 (3, 3) times, K2tog, sl 1 wyib, SSK, K32 (37, 42). **Row 4:** P across. Work 6 rows St st.

Change to CC. **Row 1:** K8 (13, 18), *[(K1, YO) 3 times, K 1] all in same st*, K19, rep from * to*, K39, rep from * to *, K9, rep from * to *, K13 (18, 23). **Row 2:** K across.

Change to MC. **Row 1:** K7 (12, 17), *K2tog, K5, SSK*, K17, rep from * to *, K37, rep from * to *, K7, rep from * to *, K12 (17, 22). **Row 2:** P12 (17, 22), *SSP, P1, sl 1 wyif, P1, P2tog*, P7, rep from * to *, P37, rep from * to *, P17, rep from * to *, P7 (12, 17). **Row 3:** K7 (12, 17), *K2tog, sl 1, wyib, SSK*, K17, rep from * to *, K37, rep from * to *, K7, rep from * to *, K12 (17, 22). **Row 4:** P across. Work 10 rows in St st.

Change to CC. **Row 1:** K38 (43, 48), *[(K1, YO) 3 times, K1] all in same st*, K19, rep from * to *, K14, rep from * to *, K18 (23, 28). **Row 2:** K across.

Change to MC. **Row 1:** K37 (42, 47), *K2tog, K5, SSK*, K17, rep from * to *, K12, rep from * to *, K17 (22, 27). **Row 2:** P17 (22, 27), *SSP, P1, sl 1 wyif, P1, P2tog*, P12, rep from * to *, P17, rep from * to *, P37 (42, 47). **Row 3:** K37 (42, 47), *K2tog, sl 1, wyib, SSK*, K17, rep from * to *, K12, rep from * to *, K17 (22, 27). **Row 4:** P across. Cont in St st in MC until piece measures 12 (12 1/2, 13)" from CO edge.

## Armhole Shaping

WITH MC, BO 8 (8, 9) sts at beg of next 2 rows. Work decs as follows on RS: K2, SSK, K to 4 sts from end, K2tog, K2, or on WS: P2, P2tog, P to 4 sts from end, SSP, P2. Dec every 3 rows 12 (6, 6) times, then EOR 12 (23, 26) times; at the same time, when there are 40 (42, 44) sts, beg neck shaping. Place center 22 (22, 24) sts on holder, work each shoulder separately, cont with armhole decs and dec 1 st at neck edge EOR 3 times. Finish off.

# FRONT

WORK AS for back until 48 (54, 56) sts remain; beg neck shaping. Place center 16 (16, 18) sts on holder, work each shoulder separately, cont with armhole decs as given for back and dec 1 st at neck edge EOR 6 (6, 6) times. Finish off.

# LEFT SLEEVE

WITH SIZE 6 needles and MC, CO 52 (62, 72) sts. Work as for border on back. Change to size 7 needles and CC, K13 (18, 23), *[(K1, YO) 3 times, K1] all in same st*, K19, rep from * to *, K18 (23, 28). **Next row:** K across.

Change to MC. **Row 1:** K12 (17, 22), *K2tog, K5, SSK*, K17, rep from * to *, K17 (22, 27). **Row 2:** P17 (22, 27), *SSP, P1, sl 1 wyif, P1, P2tog*, P17, rep from * to *, P12 (17, 22). **Row 3:** K12 (17, 22), *K2tog, sl 1 wyib, SSK*, K17, rep from * to *, K17 (22, 27). **Row 4:** P across. Work 6 rows in St st.

Change to CC. **Row 1:** K8 (13, 18), *[(K1, YO) 3 times, K1] all in same st*, K14, rep from * to *, K14, rep from * to *, K13 (18, 23). **Row 2:** K across.

Change to MC. **Row 1:** K7 (12, 17), *K2tog, K5, SSK*, K12, rep from * to *, K12, rep from * to *, K12 (17, 22). **Row 2:** P12 (17, 22), *SSP, P1, sl 1 wyif, P1, P2tog*, P12, rep from * to *, P12, rep from * to *, P7 (12, 17). **Row 3:** K7 (12, 17), *K2tog, sl 1, wyib, SSK*, K12, rep from * to *, K12, rep from * to *, K12 (17, 22). **Row 4:** P across. Work 10 rows in St st.

Change to CC. **Row 1:** K18 (23, 28), *[(K1, YO) 3 times, K1] all in same st*, K24, rep from * to *, K8 (13, 18). **Row 2:** K across.

Change to MC. **Row 1:** K17 (22, 27), *K2tog, K5, SSK*, K22, rep from * to *, K7 (12, 17). **Row 2:** P7 (12, 17), *SSP, P1, sl 1 wyif, P1, P2tog*, P22, rep from * to *, P17 (22, 27). **Row 3:** K17 (22, 27), *K2tog, sl 1, wyib, SSK*, K22, rep from * to *, K7 (12, 17). **Row 4:** P across. Cont in St st, inc 1 st at each end, every 4 (5, 5) rows until there are 72 (82, 92) sts. When sleeve measures 11½ (12, 12½)" from beg, beg raglan shaping. BO 8 (8, 9) sts at beg of next 2 rows. Dec 1 st at each end EOR 14 (24, 26) times, then every 3 rows 11 (6, 8) times. BO rem 6 (6, 6) sts.

## Right Sleeve

CO and work as for back border. Change to size 7 needles and CC, K18 (23, 28), *[(K1, YO) 3 times, K1] all in same st,* K19, rep from * to *, K13 (18, 23). **Next row:** K across.

Change to MC. **Row 1:** K17 (22, 27), *K2tog, K5, SSK*, K17, rep from * to *, K12 (17, 22). **Row 2:** P12 (17, 22), *SSP, P1, sl 1 wyif, P1, P2tog*, P17, rep from * to *, P17 (22, 27). **Row 3:** K17 (22, 27), *K2tog, sl 1 wyib, SSK*, K17, rep from * to *, K12 (17, 22). **Row 4:** P across. Work 6 rows in St st.

Change to CC. **Row 1:** K13 (18, 23), *[(K1, YO) 3 times, K1] all in same st*, K14, rep from * to *, K14, rep from * to *, K8 (13, 18). **Row 2:** K across.

Change to MC. **Row 1:** K12 (17, 22), *K2tog, K5, SSK*, K12, rep from * to *, K12, rep from * to *, K7 (12, 17). **Row 2:** P7 (12, 17), *SSP, P1, sl 1 wyif, P1, P2tog*, P12, rep from * to *, P12, rep from * to *, P12 (17, 22). **Row 3:** K12 (17, 22), *K2tog, sl 1, wyib, SSK*, K12, rep from * to *, K12, rep from * to *, K7 (12, 17). **Row 4:** P across. Work 10 rows in St st.

Change to CC. **Row 1:** K8 (13, 18), *[(K1, YO) 3 times, K1] all in same st*, K24, rep from * to *, K18 (23, 28). **Row 2:** K across.

Change to MC. **Row 1:** K7 (12, 17), *K2tog, K5, SSK*, K22, rep from * to *, K17 (22, 27). **Row 2:** P17 (22, 27), *SSP, P1, sl 1 wyif, P1, P2tog*, P22, rep from * to *, P7 (12, 17). **Row 3:** K7 (12, 17), *K2tog, sl 1 wyib, SSK*, K22, rep from * to *, K17 (22, 27). **Row 4:** P across. Cont as for left sleeve for inc and raglan shaping.

## Finishing

Weave raglan edge of sleeves to raglan edges of body of sweater.

### Neck Edge

Starting at right back raglan seam, with 16" size 6 circ needles and MC, PU 4 (4, 5) sts. K across 20 (22, 24) sts from holder, PU 4 (4, 5) sts to left back seam, PU 7 (7, 7) sts to left front seam, PU 12 (12, 14) sts to holder, K across 16 (18, 18) sts on holder, PU 12 (12, 14) sts to right front seam, PU 7 (7, 7) sts to right back seam, PM, do not turn. P 1 row, K 1 row, P 1 row, BO loosely in P.

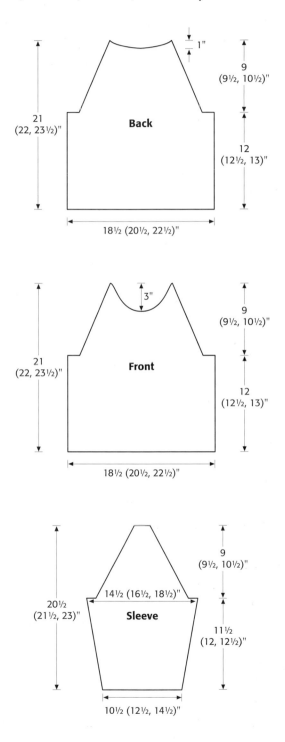

# Slip-Stitch Rainbow Cardigan

*Fall* ◆ *Beginner to Intermediate*

## KNITTED MEASUREMENTS

SIZES: Small (Medium, Large)
FINISHED BUST: 38 (42, 46)"
LENGTH: 22 (24, 26)"

## MATERIALS

◆ Limbo by Stahl Wool, distributed by Tahki
Yarns (100% superwash wool, 135yds/50g)
  - 10 (11, 12) skeins red 4555 (MC)
  - 1 (2, 2) skeins light yellow 4548 (CC1)
  - 1 (2, 2) skeins gold 4470 (CC2)
  - 1 (2, 2) skeins orange 4469 (CC3)
  - 1 (2, 2) skeins persimmon 4460 (CC4)
  - 1 (2, 2) skeins raspberry 4569 (CC5)
  - 1 (2, 2) skeins purple 4462 (CC6)

◆ Sizes 3 and 5 circular needles (29") (you need
2 of size 5), or size required to obtain gauge
◆ Size 5 circular needles (24")
◆ 4 stitch holders
◆ 4 point protectors
◆ 5 (5, 6) buttons, ¾" diameter

## GAUGE

24 sts and 48 rows = 4" in pattern on size 5 needles

NOTE: *Sweater is worked in the round without side
seams.*

# Main Pattern Stitch

**Rows 1 and 2:** K across with MC.

**Rows 3 and 4:** With designated color in sequence below, (sl 1, K1) across.

**Rows 5 and 6:** K across with MC.

**Row 7:** With designated color in sequence, K2, sl 1, (K3, sl 1), rep to last 2 sts, K2.

**Row 8:** With same color as row 7, P2, sl 1, (P3, sl 1), rep to last 2 sts, P2.

Substitute colors for each row as shown below. Cut yarns—except for MC—after end of WS rows. Carry MC loosely up side.

## Color Sequence

| Pattern repeat | Rows | Color |
| --- | --- | --- |
| 1 | 1 and 2 | MC |
|  | 3 and 4 | CC1 |
|  | 5 and 6 | MC |
|  | 7 and 8 | CC3 |
| 2 | 1 and 2 | MC |
|  | 3 and 4 | CC2 |
|  | 5 and 6 | MC |
|  | 7 and 8 | CC4 |
| 3 | 1 and 2 | MC |
|  | 3 and 4 | CC1 |
|  | 5 and 6 | MC |
|  | 7 and 8 | CC5 |
| 4 | 1 and 2 | MC |
|  | 3 and 4 | CC2 |
|  | 5 and 6 | MC |
|  | 7 and 8 | CC6 |

| Pattern repeat | Rows | Color |
| --- | --- | --- |
| 5 | 1 and 2 | MC |
|  | 3 and 4 | CC2 |
|  | 5 and 6 | MC |
|  | 7 and 8 | CC5 |
| 6 | 1 and 2 | MC |
|  | 3 and 4 | CC1 |
|  | 5 and 6 | MC |
|  | 7 and 8 | CC4 |
| 7 | 1 and 2 | MC |
|  | 3 and 4 | CC2 |
|  | 5 and 6 | MC |
|  | 7 and 8 | CC3 |
| 8 | 1 and 2 | MC |
|  | 3 and 4 | CC1 |
|  | 5 and 6 | MC |
|  | 7 and 8 | CC4 |
| 9 | 1 and 2 | MC |
|  | 3 and 4 | CC2 |
|  | 5 and 6 | MC |
|  | 7 and 8 | CC5 |
| 10 | 1 and 2 | MC |
|  | 3 and 4 | CC1 |
|  | 5 and 6 | MC |
|  | 7 and 8 | CC6 |
| 11 | 1 and 2 | MC |
|  | 3 and 4 | CC1 |
|  | 5 and 6 | MC |
|  | 7 and 8 | CC5 |
| 12 | 1 and 2 | MC |
|  | 3 and 4 | CC2 |
|  | 5 and 6 | MC |
|  | 7 and 8 | CC4 |

Work these 12 pattern repeats as needed to achieve desired length.

# Ribbing Pattern

**Row 1 (WS):** K1, P2, (K2, P2) to last st, K1.
**Row 2:** P1, K2, (P2, K2) to last st, P1.

# Body

With 29" size 3 needles, CO 228 (260, 278) sts; do not join. Work ribbing pattern for 2 (2¼, 2½)". On last WS row, inc 1 st—229 (261, 279) sts. Change to 29" size 5 needles and work patt to end of patt rep 4—32 rows.

## Beg Slash Pockets on Right Front

Starting on row 33 of right front, with 24" size 5 needles, work next patt row on first 45 (51, 55) sts, leave rem sts on longer needle. Place point protectors on needles. Dec 1 st at end of every RS row, keeping in patt until there are 18 (24, 28) sts, end with row 1. Leave on needle, place point protectors on needles.

## Back

Working on the next 139 (159, 169) sts, beg color sequence at row 1 of patt rep 5. Place rem sts on other 29" size 5 needles. Place point protectors on needles. Inc 1 st at beg and end of row on every RS row, keeping continuity of patt until there are 193 (213, 223) sts, end with row 1. Leave sts on needles. Place point protectors on needles.

## Beg Slash Pockets on Left Front

Working on 45 (51, 55) sts, beg color sequence at row 1 of patt rep 5. Dec 1 st at beg of every RS row, keeping in patt until there are 18 (24, 28) sts, end with row 1.

## Rejoin Fronts and Back

With 29" size 5 needles, which should be attached to knitting for left front, turn and work the next WS row, a row 2, rejoining the fronts and the back. All sts should be in same pattern and sequence before slash pockets were made—229 (261, 279) sts. Cont in patt until body measures 13 (14, 15)" from the beg; end with WS row. Then divide for armholes as follows.

## Right Front

With other 29" size 5 needles, work across 49 (57, 63) sts of right front. Leave rem sts on needle; place point protectors on needles. Cont in patt, dec 1 st at neck edge on rows 2 and 6 of patt, keeping continuity of patt, until there are 21 (25, 27) sts. When armhole measures 9 (10, 11)", end with a row 2 or 6; place shoulder sts on holder. Cut yarns.

## Back

Reattach MC at right underarm with RS facing, BO 15 sts for armhole. Beg patt for that row, joining appropriate second color as needed and working across 101 (117, 123) sts. Place last 64 (72, 78) sts on 24" size 5 needles; place point protectors on needles. Cont on back until armhole measures ¾" less than front armhole. **Shape back neck:** Work across row, BO center 59 (67, 69) sts, finish row. Working each side separately on 21 (25, 27) sts, cont until back measures same as front; end on the same row as front. Place shoulder sts on holder.

## Left Front

Reattach MC at left underarm with RS facing, BO 15 sts for armhole. Beg patt for that row, joining appropriate second color as needed; work as for right front, reversing shaping. Place shoulder sts on holder.

## SLEEVES

WITH 29" size 3 needles, cast on 44 (48, 58) sts. Work ribbing patt for 2 (2¼, 2½)", inc 27 (27, 21) sts evenly across last row—71 (75, 79) sts. Change to 24" size 5 circ needles and work patt as for body of sweater; starting on row 5 and then every 8 rows, inc 1 st at each end, working inc into patt, until there are 109 (119, 133) sts. End with row 1 or 6 when sleeve measures 17½ (18, 19½)" or desired length. BO all sts.

## FINISHING

PLACE SHOULDER sts on size 5 needles, and with RS tog, work 3-needle BO. Weave sleeve seam, leaving about a 1" opening at top to fit bound-off area of underarm. Weave sleeve into armhole, fitting the sleeve into the armhole area, matching the 1" opening of sleeve seam to bound-off sts of armhole.

### Pockets

WITH 24" SIZE 5 needles and CC6, PU 40 sts along back edge of slash pocket. Work in St st, dec 1 st at each end EOR. Finish off when 1 st remains. Sew pockets to inside of sweater, being careful pocket area remains flat. Rep for other pocket.

### Pocket Bands

WITH RS facing, size 3 needles, and MC, PU 51 sts along outer edge of pocket. Work rows 1 through 6 of pattern with CC2 for contrast. Dec 3 sts on row 6. Work ribbing in MC as for body of sweater for 1". BO loosely.

### Front Band

WITH RS facing, size 3 needles, and MC, PU 18 sts in ribbing, 60 (66, 72) sts to start of V neck, 70 (76, 82) sts to right shoulder seam, 55 (63, 65) sts across back neck, 70 (76, 82) sts to start of V neck, 60 (66, 72) sts on left front, and 18 sts in ribbing—351 (383, 409) sts. Work rows 1 through 6 of patt using CC1 for contrast. Dec 3 sts across back neck on row 6. Work ribbing as for body of sweater. On fourth row of ribbing, work buttonholes as follows: Work in rib for 10 (10, 10) sts, BO 2 sts, *work in rib for 14 (16, 16) sts, BO 2 sts*; rep from * to * 3 (3, 4) times, finish row. On next row, cont in ribbing, CO 2 sts over 2 BO sts of previous row. Cont in ribbing for 3 more rows. BO loosely. Block gently if needed. Do not over steam slip stitches. They should appear slightly raised. Sew on buttons.

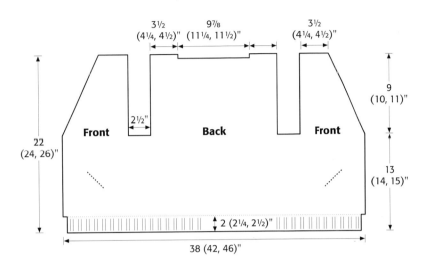

3½
(4¼, 4½)"    9⅞
(11¼, 11½)"    3½
(4¼, 4½)"

9
(10, 11)"

**Front**    2½"    **Back**    **Front**

22
(24, 26)"    13
(14, 15)"

2 (2¼, 2½)"

38 (42, 46)"

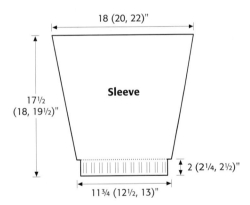

18 (20, 22)"

**Sleeve**

17½
(18, 19½)"

2 (2¼, 2½)"

11¾ (12½, 13)"

# Cotton Slip-Stitch Pullover

*Summer* ♦ *Beginner to Intermediate*

## KNITTED MEASUREMENTS

SIZES: Petite, Small, Medium, and Large
FINISHED BUST: 35 (38, 44, 47)"
LENGTH: 20½ (21, 22, 22½)"

## MATERIALS

- 12 (13, 14, 16) skeins Cotton Classic by Tahki (100% cotton, 108yds/50g), color 3754
- Sizes 5 and 6 circular needles (24"), or size required to obtain gauge
- Ring marker

## GAUGE

22 sts and 40 rows = 4" in main pattern stitch on size 6 needles

## RIB PATTERN STITCH

**Row 1 (WS):** K2, *(P1, K1) twice, P1, K3*; rep from * to * to last 2 sts, K2.
**Row 2:** K3, *P1, K1, P1, K5*; rep from * to * to last 3 sts, K3.

## Main Pattern Stitch

For gauge swatch, CO 33 sts.

**Rows 1 and 3 (WS):** K2, *P5, K3*, rep from * to *, end K2.

**Row 2:** K2, *sl 5 wyif, float yarn loosely across the 5 sts, K3*, rep from * to *, end K2 (1).

**Row 4:** K4, *insert needle under loose strand created in row 2, then into st on needle, K tog with st on needle (2), K7*, rep from * to *, end K4.

Rep rows 1–4.

## Back

With size 5 needles, CO 97 (105, 121, 129) sts. work rib pattern stitch for 2 (2¼, 2½, 2¾)", end with row 2. Change to size 6 needles and work main pattern stitch until piece measures 11½ (12, 12½, 13)" from CO edge.

### Armhole Shaping

BO 9 (9, 15, 15) sts at beg of next 2 rows—79 (87, 91, 99) sts. Cont in patt until 5 (5, 5½, 5½)" from beg of armhole shaping.

### Back Neck Shaping

Work across 20 (22, 22, 24) sts in patt, BO center 39, (43, 47, 51) sts, finish row. Working each shoulder separately, dec 1 st at neck edge EOR twice—18 (20, 20, 22) sts each shoulder. Cont in patt until armhole measures 9 (9, 9½, 9½)". BO all sts.

## Front

Work as for back until armhole measures 4 (4, 4½, 4½)" from beg of armhole shaping.

### Front Neck Shaping

Work across 28 (30, 30, 32) sts in patt, BO center 23 (27, 31, 35) sts, finish row. Work each shoulder separately, dec 1 st at neck edge EOR 10 times—18 (20, 20, 22) sts each shoulder. Cont in patt until armhole measures same as back. BO all sts.

## Sleeves

With size 5 needles, CO 81 (81, 89, 89) sts. Work rib pattern stitch for 1¼ (1½, 1½, 1¾)", end with row 2. Change to size 6 needles and beg main pattern stitch, inc 1 st at each edge every 4 rows 10 times, keep inc sts in garter st—101 (101, 109, 109) sts. When sleeve measures 5¾ (6, 6¼, 6½)", BO all sts.

## Finishing

Weave tog shoulder seams. **Neckband:** Using size 5 needles, starting at right shoulder seam, PU 17 (18, 18, 20) sts to BO edge of back, PU 38 (44, 44, 48) sts across BO edge, 17 (18, 18, 20) sts to left shoulder seam, 32 (34, 36, 38) sts to front BO edge, 24 (28, 32, 36) sts across BO sts, 32 (34, 36, 38) sts to right shoulder seam, PM, join. Work circular rib patt as follows: **Round 1:** *(K1, P1) twice, K4*, rep from * to * to marker. **Round 2:** *(K1, P1) twice, K1, P3*, rep from * to * to marker. Rep 1st and 2nd rounds, 3 (3, 4, 4) more times. **Next round:** *(K1, P1) twice, K1, K2tog, K1*, rep from * to * to marker. **Next round:** *(K1, P1) twice, K1, P2*, rep from

* to * to marker. **Next round:** *(K1, P1) twice, K3*, rep from * to * to marker. Rep last 2 rows 2 (2, 3, 3) more times. **Next round:** *(K1, P1) twice, K1, K2tog*, rep from * to * to marker. BO in patt on next row.

Weave sleeve and side seams. Mist with water, smooth, and lay flat to dry.

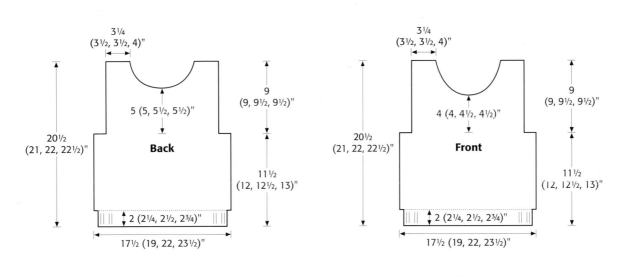

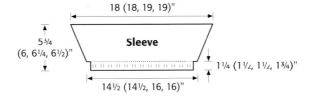

# Jewel-Toned Mosaic-Stitch Pullover

## Winter ♦ Intermediate

## KNITTED MEASUREMENTS

SIZES: Small (Medium, Large)
FINISHED BUST: 34 (40, 45)"
LENGTH: 22 (23½, 25)"

## MATERIALS

♦ Canaan Mohair (100% merino wool,
300yds/100g)
  · 1 (2, 2) skeins Hunter Green 214
  · 1 (2, 2) skeins Cranberry 206
  · 1 (2, 2) skeins Peacock 205
  · 1 (2, 2) skeins Aubergine 214
♦ Sizes 6 and 7 straight needles, or size required
to obtain gauge
♦ Size 6 circular needles (24")
♦ Ring markers

## GAUGE

20 sts and 40 rows = 4" in pattern stitch on size 7
needles

For gauge swatch: CO 44 with size 7 needles and
color A (see color sequence chart on page 34), work
rows 1 through 14 of pattern stitch 4 times, changing
colors as given in chart.

## PATTERN STITCH

*(Multiple of 14 plus 2 sts)*
**Rows 1, 5, and 9 (RS):** With color B (see color
sequence chart on page 34), K1 *K7, (sl 1, K1) 3
times, sl 1*; rep from * to *, end K1.
**Row 2 and all wrong-side rows not given in
directions:** Knit the same sts worked on the previous row with the same color. Slip all the sts that
were slipped on the RS row wyib.
**Rows 3, 7, and 11:** With color A (see color
sequence chart on page 34, K1, *(sl 1, K1) 3 times,
sl 1, K7*; rep from * to *, end K1.
**Rows 13 and 14:** K with next color A.
Rep these 14 rows for the entire sweater in color
sequence indicated in chart on page 34.

## Color sequence chart

|  | Color A | Color B |
|---|---|---|
| First repeat, rows 1 thru 12 | Hunter | Cranberry |
| *Second repeat, rows 13 and 14 and 1 thru 12 | Cranberry | Peacock |
| Third repeat, rows 13 and 14 and 1 thru 12 | Peacock | Aubergine |
| Fourth repeat, rows 13 and 14 and 1 thru 12 | Aubergine | Hunter |
| Fifth repeat, rows 13 and 14 and 1 thru 12 | Hunter | Cranberry* |
| Rep color sequence from * to * for entire sweater. | | |

## BACK

WITH HUNTER and size 6 straight needles, CO 81 (95, 109) sts. K 5 rows, on last row inc 5 sts evenly across—86 (100, 114) sts. Change to size 7 needles, work in patt and beg color sequence as indicated above. When work measures 13 (14, 15)" from beg, BO 14 sts at beg of next 2 rows, cont in patt until armhole measures 9 (9½, 10)". BO all sts. Keep track of row you ended on, so you can end front on the same row.

## FRONT

WORK AS for back until armhole measures 6 (6, 6½)". Shape neck as follows: work across 9 (16, 23) sts in patt, BO center 40 sts, finish row in patt. Work both sides separately until armholes measure 9 (9½, 10)", ending with same row as back. BO all sts.

## SLEEVES

WITH SIZE 6 needles and Hunter, CO 40 (40, 54) sts. K 5 rows, on last row inc 4 sts evenly across the row—44 (44, 58) sts. Change to size 7 needles, beg patt in color sequence, inc 1 st at each end on row 5 and then every 6 rows. Keep edge st at each end in K. Place marker after first st and before last st for inc placement. Make inc before first marker and after last marker, working incs into patt sts until there are 90 (96, 100) sts. Use the chart below to assist with sleeve increases. The inc row number is listed on the left; the number of sts you should have outside of the ring markers is on the right. Cross out each number on the right side of chart as you work that inc. When sleeve measures 20 (21, 22)", BO all sts.

## Increase chart for sleeves

| Increase rows | Number of sts outside of markers on each end | | | |
|---|---|---|---|---|
| In pattern | 1st | 2nd | 3rd | 4th repeat of inc rows |
| 5 | 2 | 9 | 16 | 23 (100 sts total; stop incs for large) |
| 11 | 3 | 10 | 17 | 24 (90 sts total; stop incs for small) |
| 3 | 4 | 11 | 18 | 25 |
| 9 | 5 | 12 | 19 | 26 |
| 1 | 6 | 13 | 20 | 27 (96 sts total; stop incs for medium) |
| 7 | 7 | 14 | 21 | |
| 13 | 8 | 15 | 22 | |

When you reach the appropriate number of sts for your size, work even until sleeve measures 20 (21, 22)". BO all sts.

# FINISHING

## Seams

WEAVE TOG shoulder seams. Dampen and lay flat, pinning to correct measurements. Do not remove until dry. Weave side and sleeve seams.

## Neck

WITH SIZE 6 circ needles and Hunter, starting at right shoulder seam, PU 40 sts across back neck, PM, PU 14 (15, 16) sts down left front, PM, PU 40 sts across front neck, PM, PU 14 (15, 16) sts up right neck, PM. Join. **Row 1:** Purl. **Row 2:** *K2 tog, K to 2 sts before marker, K2tog, slip marker, rep from * to * around. Rep rows 1 and 2 one more time. BO loosely in purl.

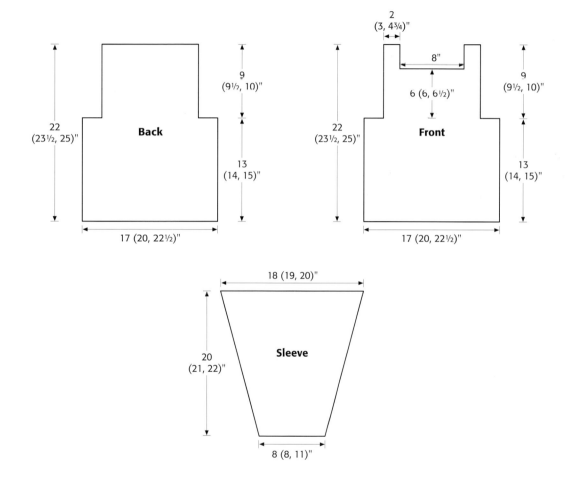

# Interlocking Squares

INTERLOCKING SQUARES AND DIAMONDS is a fascinating technique in knitting today. Simple squares and diamonds are planned using graph paper. The size of a garment is determined by the number of stitches in a motif (square or diamond). If the patterns are not exactly the size you need, you can alter the size by changing the size of the motif. If your sample of a stockinette-stitch diamond measures 4" across and there are 10 diamonds across the body of the garment, the piece will end up 40" across. If you want to change the size slightly, either up or down, knit another motif over more or fewer stitches or on a smaller or bigger needle to achieve your desired size. Multiply the measurement by 10 to determine the width of the knitted piece. Remember: if you change the size across the motif, you are also changing the length, so you might need to add or subtract rows of squares or diamonds to account for this. All the shaping involved in creating necks and armholes is done by eliminating squares or diamonds.

You need to do almost no sewing when these garments are finished. You will knit together all the squares and diamonds as they are worked. They can be worked in any order as long as the appropriate areas to pick up stitches already exist. The patterns will have lots of ends, but you don't need to weave them in after knitting each motif. You can knit them in as you add new yarn (see page 11), so when the sweaters come off the needles, they need a minimal amount of finishing.

# and Diamonds

All the designs have a chart to follow. The chart indicates which yarns to use and where to work the motifs. It is easy to lose your place when following the charts, so mark off the motifs as you make them. In the case of the Pinwheel Vest, the square and diamonds *have* to be worked in the order given so there is no break in the construction of the garment. You might have difficulty figuring out where you are if you make the motifs out of order.

The motifs utilize 2 different types of decreases for the center, depending on whether you are knitting a garter-stitch square or a stockinette-stitch diamond. Read the instructions carefully so you don't confuse them.

You construct garter-stitch squares by picking up the appropriate number of stitches on the right side and working garter stitch with a decrease over the middle 3 stitches on the right side. The total number of stitches must be odd so you end with 1 stitch to finish off. For example, cast on 19 stitches. Row 1 (WS): K across. Row 2: K to center 3 sts, in this case K8, sl 1 st as if to purl, K2tog, pass the sl st over, K rem 8 sts. Rep these 2 rows, working 1 less stitch before and after the center dec on every row 2 until 1 st remains. Finish off last st.

You work interlocking diamonds in a similar manner, except that the center 3 stitches on a full diamond are worked using a central chain decrease (see page 12). There are 5 variations on the diamond shape required for the projects. They are described on the next 2 pages. Each motif will end with a stitch on a pin, unless otherwise directed.

## MAIN DIAMOND PATTERN

With RS facing, and starting at top of a diamond, PU appropriate number of sts down the left side of the diamond on the right, K the st on the pin, then remove pin and PU appropriate number of sts up the right side of the adjacent diamond on the left. *Turn, P across. On RS rows: K to center 3 sts, work CCD (see page 12), finish row on WS rows, P across. Cont with these 2 rows until 1 st rem, place last st on pin.*

## BEGINNING DIAMOND

CO appropriate number of sts, work from * to * of main diamond pattern. Place last st on pin.

## RIGHT HALF DIAMOND

With RS facing, PU appropriate number of sts along right edge of adjacent diamond. Do not use st on pin at top of diamond. *Turn, P across, turn, K1, SSK, K to end.* Rep from * to *, working 1 less st after dec until 2 sts remain, turn, P2tog, place last st on pin.

## LEFT HALF DIAMOND

With RS facing, PU appropriate number of sts on left edge of adjacent diamond. Do not use st on pin at top of diamond. *Turn, P across, turn, K to last 3 sts, K2tog, K1.* Rep from * to *, working 1 less st before dec until 2 sts remain, turn, P2tog, place last st on pin.

## TOP HALF DIAMOND

Pick up as for main diamond on appropriate edges of diamonds. *Turn, P across. Turn, SSK, K to center 3 sts, work CCD, K to 2 sts from the end, K2tog.* Rep from * to *, keeping CCD on center 3 sts until 5 sts remain, SSK, K1, K2tog, turn, P3tog, finish off.

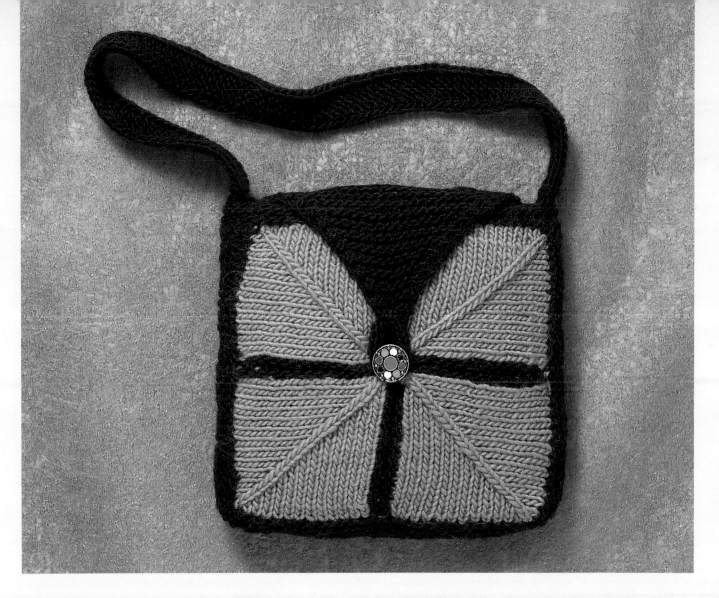

# Pinwheel Purse

## KNITTED MEASUREMENTS

9" wide by 9" high by 2" deep

## MATERIALS

- Lamb's Pride Worsted Weight Yarn by Brown Sheep (85% wool, 15% mohair, 190yds/114g)
  - 1 skein limeade M120 (MC)
  - 1 skein sapphire M65 (CC)
- Size 9 circular needle (24"), or size required to obtain gauge
- 3 size 8 double-pointed needles
- ½ yd. fabric for lining
- ½ yd. Pellon Craft-Fuse
- 1 button, 1¼" diameter

## GAUGE

1 diamond = 5" across widest point on size 9 needles

# Stockinette-Stitch Diamond (SSD)

CO 27 sts, P back, K12, work CCD, K12, P back, K11, work CCD, K11, P back, K10, work CCD, K10, P back, K9, work CCD, K9, P back, K8, work CCD, K8, P back, K7, work CCD, K7, P back, K6, work CCD, K6, P back, K5, work CCD, K5, P back, K4, work CCD, K4, P back, K3, work CCD, K3, P back, K2, work CCD, K2, P back, K1, work CCD, K1, P back, work CCD, finish off, do not weave in end.

# Garter-Stitch Square (GSS)

CO 15 sts, K back, K6, sl 1, K2tog, psso, K6, K back, K5, sl 1, K2tog, psso, K5, K back, K4, sl 1, K2tog, psso, K4, K back, K3, sl 1, K2tog, psso, K3, K back, K2, sl 1, K2tog, psso, K2, K back, K1, sl 1, K2tog, psso, K1, K back, sl 1, K2tog, psso, finish off or beg new GSS, as directed.

# Front

With size 9 needles and MC, K 4 SSDs as directed above. Arrange the SSDs as shown and number them 1a, 2a, 3a, and 4a. The diagram shows the direction of the knitting and designates where the center dec of the diamond is located.

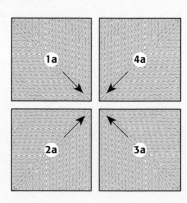

## Joining SSDs

Knit SSDs together as follows: * RS of SSDs facing, with size 8 dpn and CC, PU 14 sts on bottom of SSD 1a, K back. Set aside. With another size 8 dpn, PU 14 sts on top of SSD 2a, K back (1). With WS together and third size 8 dpn, knit tog the 2 pieces using 3-needle BO (2). (See page 10.) Finish off.* Rep from * to * using right side of SSD 2a and the left side of SSD 3a. Rep from * to * using the top of SSD 3a and the bottom of SSD 4a. Rep from * to * using the left side of SSD 4a and the right side of SSD 1a. Join points together using one of the tails from the diamonds. Weave in all ends. Trace shape of front on a piece of paper to use for lining pattern later.

# Sides and Bottom

**GSS 1b:** RS SSDs facing, with size 9 needles and CC, starting on left edge of SSD 1a, CO 7 sts, PU 8 sts halfway down SSD 1a. **GSS 2b:** PU 7 sts across bottom of GSS 1b, 1 st in corner and 7 sts on second half of SSD 1a. **GSS 3b:** PU 7 sts across bottom of GSS 2b, 1 st in corner and 7 sts on first half of SSD 2a. **GSS 4b:** PU 7 sts on bottom of GSS 3b, 1 st in corner, and 7 stitches across 2nd half of SSD 2a. **GSS 5b:** PU 7 sts on bottom of GSS 4b, 1 st at corner, and 7 sts on first half of bottom of SSD 2a. Arrow on diagram shows corner. **GSS 6b:** PU 7 sts on side of GSS 5b, 1 st in corner and 7 sts on 2nd half of SSD 2a. **GSS 7b:** PU 7 sts on side of GSS 6b, 1 st in corner and 7 sts on first half of SSD 3a. **GSS 8b:** PU 7 sts on side of GSS 7b, 1 st in corner, and 7 sts across last half of SSD 3a. **GSS 9b:** PU 7 sts across edge of GSS 8b, 1 st in corner, and 7 sts across first half of side of SSD 3a. Arrow on diagram shows corner. **GSS 10b:** PU 7 sts across top of GSS 9b, 1 st in corner, and 7 sts across top half of SSD 3a. **GSS 11b:** PU 7 st across top of GSS 10b, 1 st in corner and 7 sts across first half of SSD 4a. **GSS 12b:** PU 7 sts across top of GSS 11b, 1 st in corner, and 7 sts across last half of SSD 4a. Do not finish off, place last stitch on right needle, pick up 43 more stitches across top of 12b, 4a, 1a, and 1b. K 3 rows. Work 2-st I-cord BO (see page 10). Measure the sides and bottom and trace the shape on a piece of paper to use as a lining pattern later.

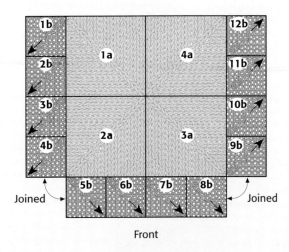

Front

## BACK

**SSD 5a:** RS of GSS 1b and 2b facing, with size 9 needles and MC, CO 14 sts, PU 13 sts down edge of GSS 1b and 2b. **SSD 6a:** PU 13 sts down edge of GSS 3b and 4b, 1 st in corner, and 13 sts across top of GSS 5b and 6b. **SSD 7a:** PU 13 sts across top of GSS 7b and 8b, 1 st in corner, and 13 sts up

edge of GSS 9b and 10b. **SSD 8a:** PU 13 sts up edge of GSS 11b and 12b, CO 14 sts.

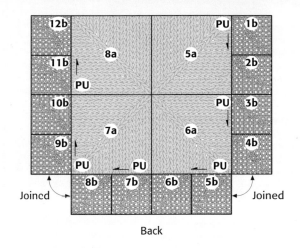

Back

## FINISHING

### *Flap*

HOLD KNITTING with RS facing. With size 9 needles, PU 27 sts across top of back. K every row for 1½". Shape flap as follows: **Row 1:** K1, SSK, K to last 3 sts, K2tog, K1. **Row 2:** K across. Rep these 2 rows until 5 sts remain. K1, Sl 1, K2tog, psso, K1; 3 sts remain. K across. Work 3" of I cord. (See page 11.) BO. Fold into loop and sew as shown in photo to form button loop.

### *Strap*

WITH SIZE 8 dpn and CC, PU 8 sts across top of left side edge. **Row 1:** P2, K4, sl 2 wyif. **Row 2:** K to last 2 sts, sl 2 wyib. Rep these 2 rows for 24" or to desired length, ending with row 1. **Next row:** K2tog, K4, K2tog. BO all sts. Sew to right side edge.

See "Lining Purses" (page 124) for lining instructions. Sew on button.

# Multiple Size—Squares Vest

*Summer* ♦ *Beginner*

## KNITTED MEASUREMENTS

SIZES: Small (Medium, Large)
FINISHED BUST: 39½ (44, 49)"
LENGTH: 20 (22, 24¼)"

## MATERIALS

♦ 7 skeins Fizz by Trendsetter Yarns (30% cotton, 38% polyamide, 32% acrylic, 96yds/50g), color 961 (MC)
♦ 4 skeins Aura by Trendsetter Yarns (100% nylon, 135yds/50g), color 8262 (CC)
♦ Sizes 7 and 8 needles, or size required to obtain gauge
♦ 4 buttons, ½" diameter

## GAUGE

SMALL SQUARE worked over 19 (21, 23) sts = 1⅞ (2, 2¼)" on size 8 needles

NOTE: *Do not cut yarns. Float them loosely up the edge of the work.*

## SMALL SQUARE (SS)

*Use size 7 needles for borders and size 8 needles in body.*

WITH SIZE 8 needles and MC, CO 19 (21, 23) sts or PU sts as given in the directions, K 1 row. Change to CC (RS), K8 (9, 10), sl 1 st, K2tog, psso. K to end. K 1 row. Change to MC, K7 (8, 9), sl 1 st, K2tog, psso. K to end. K 1 row. Change to CC, K6 (8, 9), sl 1 st, K2tog, psso. K to end. K 1 row. Proceed in this manner, working 1 st less to center, work dec, and K to end. K 1 row in same color; alternate colors every 2 rows. When there are 3 sts on RS, sl 1, K2tog, psso, finish off. Work all small squares in this color sequence.

## Medium Square (MS)

With size 8 needles and MC, CO or PU sts as given in the directions—37 (41, 45) sts. K 1 row. (RS) K17 (19, 21) sts, sl 1 st, K2tog, psso. K to end. K 1 row. K16 (18, 20) sts, sl 1 st, K2tog, psso. K to end. K 1 row. K15 (17, 19) sts, sl 1 st, K2tog, psso. K to end. K 1 row. Change to CC, K15 (17, 19) sts, sl 1 st, K2tog, psso. K to end. K 1 row. K14 (16, 18) sts, sl 1 st, K2tog, psso. K to end. K 1 row. Proceed in this manner, working 1 st less to center, work dec, and K to end. K 1 row in same color, alternate colors every 4 rows. When down to 3 sts on RS, sl 1, K2tog, psso, finish off. Work all medium squares in this color sequence.

## Large Square (LS)

With size 8 needles and designated color, CO or PU sts as given in the directions—99 (101, 111) sts. K1 row, using color as directed below, K48 (49, 54) sts, sl 1 st, K2tog, psso. K to end. K 1 row. Change colors as directed in pattern. (RS) K47 (48, 53), sl 1 st, K2tog, psso. K to end. K 1 row. Working 1 st less to center, work dec, K to end. K 1 row in same color. Work all large squares in this manner, alternating colors as indicated.

**Notes on reading the chart (page 47):** The arrows show the direction of the knitting, and designate the direction of the decreases in the square. The name of the square (SS, MS, or LS) will tell you what square to make. PU and CO as directed, then follow the directions above for making the appropriate square. PU all stitches with RS facing.

Use size 7 knitting needles for small squares in border, 1–11, 53–57, and 59–63. Use size 8 needles for small squares in body and all medium and large squares.

Use cable cast on (see page 7) when casting on stitches after stitches have been picked up.

## Back

**SS 1:** With size 7 needles, CO 19 (21, 23) sts. **SS 2:** Turn SS 1 to the left so line of decreases matches arrow on diagram. PU 10 (11,12) sts on left edge of SS 1, CO 9 (10, 11) sts. **SS 3:** PU 10 (11, 12) sts on left edge of SS 2, CO 9 (10, 11) sts. **SS 4:** PU 10 (11, 12) sts on left edge of SS 3, CO 9 (10, 11) sts. **SS 5:** PU 10 (11, 12) sts on left edge of SS 4, CO 9 (10, 11) sts. **SS 6:** PU 10 (11, 12) sts on left edge of SS 5, CO 9 (10, 11) sts. **SS 7:** PU 10 (11, 12) sts on left edge of SS 6, CO 9 (10, 11) sts. **SS 8:** PU 10 (11, 12) sts on left edge of SS 7, CO 9 (10, 11) sts. **SS 9:** PU 10 (11, 12) sts on left edge of SS 8, CO 9 (10, 11) sts. **SS 10:** PU 10 (11, 12) sts on left edge of SS 9, CO 9 (10, 11) sts. **SS 11:** PU 10 (11, 12) sts on left edge of SS 10, CO 9 (10, 11) sts. **SS 12:** Change to size 8 needles, PU 10 (11, 12) sts on top edge of SS 6, CO 9 (10, 11) sts. **SS 13:** CO 9 (10, 11) sts, PU 10 (11, 12) sts on top of SS 12. **SS 14:** PU 10 (11, 12) sts on top of 13, CO 9 (10, 11) sts. **SS 15:** CO 9 (10, 11) sts, PU 10 (11, 12) sts on top of SS 14. **SS 16:** PU 10 (11, 12) sts on top of SS 15, CO 9 (10, 11) sts. **LS 17:** With CC, PU 45 (50, 55) sts down left edge of SS 16, 15, 14, 13, and 12, 1 st in corner, and 45 (50, 55) sts across top of SS 7, 8, 9, 10, and 11. K back. Work LS using the following repeats of the 2 colors: 4 rows CC, *2 rows MC, 2 rows CC, 2 rows MC, 4 rows CC, 2 rows MC, 2 rows CC, 6 rows CC*. Rep from * to * 2 more times, work rem sts, alternating colors every 2 rows. **LS 18:** With MC, PU 45 (50, 55) sts across top of SS 1, 2, 3, 4, and 5, 1 st in corner, and 45 (50, 55) sts up right edge of SS 12, 13, 14, 15, and 16. Work LS using the following repeats of the 2 colors: 2 rows MC, *2 rows CC, 2 rows MC, 2 rows CC, 4 rows MC, 4 rows CC, 4 rows MC, 4 rows CC, 2 rows MC.* Rep from * to * until all sts are gone. **MS 19:** CO 19 (21, 23) sts, count over 8 (9, 10) ridges from the right edge of LS 18 and PU 18 (20, 22) sts. **MS 20:** PU 18 (20, 22) sts on left edge of MS 19, 1 st in corner, and 18 (20, 22) sts on rem sts of LS 18. **MS 21:** CO 19 (21, 23) sts, PU 18 (20,

22) sts on top of MS 19. **MS 22:** PU 18 (20, 22) sts on left edge of MS 21, 1 st in corner, and 18 (20, 22) sts on top of MS 20. **SS 23:** PU 9 (10, 11) sts, starting halfway down left edge of MS 20, 1 st in corner, and 9 (10, 11) sts on top of SS 16. **SS 24:** PU 9 (10, 11) sts, starting at top half of MS 20, 1 st in corner, and 9 (10, 11) sts on top of SS 23. **SS 25:** PU 9 (10, 11) sts, starting halfway down left edge of MS 22, 1 st in corner, and 9 (10, 11) sts on top of SS 24. **SS 26:** PU 9 (10, 11) sts, starting at top half of MS 22, 1 st in corner, and 9 (10, 11) sts on top of SS 25. **MS 27:** PU 18 (20, 22) sts on left edge of SS 24 and 23, 1 st in corner, and first 18 (20, 22) sts of LS 17. **MS 28:** PU 18 (20, 22) sts on left edge of MS 27, 1 st in corner, and next 18 (20, 22) sts of LS 17 [there should be 8 (9, 10) sts (ridges) left to pick up on LS 17]. **MS 29:** PU 18 (20, 22) sts on left edge of SS 26 and 25, 1 st in corner, and 18 (20, 22) sts on top of MS 27. **MS 30:** PU 18 (20, 22) sts on left edge of MS 29, 1 st in corner, and 18 (20, 22) sts on top of MS 28. **MS 31:** CO 19 (21, 23) sts and PU 18 (20, 22) sts on top of MS 21. **SS 32:** PU 9 (10, 11) sts halfway down left edge of MS 31, 1 st in corner, and 9 (10, 11) sts on top half of MS 22. **SS 33:** PU 9 (10, 11) sts on left edge of SS 32, 1 st in corner, and 9 (10, 11) sts on last top half of MS 22. **SS 34:** PU 9 (10, 11) sts on left edge of SS 33, 1 st in corner, and 9 (10, 11) sts on top of SS 26. **SS 35:** PU 9 (10, 11) sts on SS 34, 1 st in corner, and 9 (10, 11) sts on top half of MS 29. **SS 36:** PU 9 (10, 11) sts on SS 35, 1 st in corner, and 9 (10, 11) sts on last top half of MS 29. **SS 37:** CO 10 (11, 12) sts, PU 9 (10,11) sts on top of SS 36. **MS 38:** PU 18 (20, 22) sts on left edge of SS 37 and 36, 1 st in corner, and 18 (20, 22) sts on top of SS 30. **SS 39:** PU 9 (10, 11) sts on left edge of top half of MS 31, 1 st in corner, and 9 (10, 11) sts on top of SS 32.

## Front

**MS 40:** CO 19 (21, 23) sts and PU 18 (20, 22) sts on top of MS 31. **SS 41:** PU 9 (10, 11) sts on bottom half of MS 40, 1 st in corner, and 9 (10, 11) sts on top half of SS 39. **SS 42:** PU 9 (10, 11) sts on left side of MS 40, 1 st in corner, and 9 (10, 11) sts on top of SS 41. **SS 43:** CO 10 (11, 12) sts, PU 9 (10,11) sts on top of SS 37. **SS 44:** CO 10 (11, 12) sts, PU 9 (10,11) sts on top of SS 43. **MS 45:** PU 18 (20, 22) sts on left edge of SS 44 and 43, 1 st in corner, and 18 (20, 22) sts on top of MS 38. **MS 46:** CO 19 (21, 23) sts and PU 18 (20, 22) sts on top of MS 40. **MS 47:** PU 18 (20, 22) sts on left edge of MS 46, 1 st in corner, and 9 (10, 11) sts on SS 42, CO 9 (10, 11) sts. **Half square 48:** Turn work so back is away from you. With MC, PU 9 (10, 11) sts on top of MS 47, 1 st in corner, and 9 (10, 11) sts on edge of MS 42. SSK, K to last 2 sts, K2tog. **Next and all RS rows:** K to center 3 sts, sl 1, K2tog, psso, K to end. Rep these 2 rows until there are 3 sts left, work dec on RS. **MS 49:** Turn work so back is toward you. With MC, CO 28 (31, 34) sts, PU 9 (10, 11) sts on top of SS 44. **MS 50:** PU 18 (20, 22) sts on left edge of MS 49, 1 st in corner, and 18 (20, 22) sts on top of MS 45. **Half square 51:** Turn work so back is away from you. With MC, PU 9 (10, 11) sts on right side of SS 44, 1 st in corner, and 9 (10, 11) sts on top half of MS 49. Work as for half square 48.

## Join Front and Back at Side Seam

**LS 52:** With MC, PU 45 (50, 55) sts, starting at bottom edge of LS 18, CO 10 (11, 12) sts, PU 36 (40, 44) sts across top of MS 46 and 47, K 1 row. Work as for LS 17. Change to size 7 needles to work SSs for border. **SS 53:** PU 9 (10, 11) sts on SS 1, 1 st in corner, and 9 (10, 11) sts on first 9 (10, 11) ridges of LS 52. **SS 54:** PU 9 (10, 11) sts on SS 53, 1 st in corner, and 9 (10, 11) sts on next 9 (10, 11) ridges of LS 52. **SS 55:** PU 9 (10, 11) sts on SS 54, 1 st in corner, and 9 (10, 11) sts on next 9 (10, 11) ridges of LS 52. **SS 56:** PU 9 (10, 11) sts on SS 55, 1 st in corner, and 9 (10, 11) sts on next 9 (10, 11) ridges of LS 52. **SS 57:** PU 9 (10, 11) sts on SS 56, 1 st in corner, and 9 (10, 11) sts on next 9 (10, 11) ridges of LS 52. **LS 58:** With size 8 needles and CC, PU 36 (40, 44) sts on bottom edge of MS 49 and 50, CO 10 (11, 12) sts, PU 45 (50, 55) sts on LS 17. K 1 row. Work as for LS 18. Change to size 7 needles to work SSs for border. **SS 59:** PU 9 (10, 11) sts on last 9 (10, 11) ridges of LS 58, 1 st in corner, and 9 (10, 11) sts on SS 11. **SS 60:** PU 9 (10, 11) sts on next 9 (10, 11) ridges of LS 58, 1 st in corner, and 9 (10, 11) sts on SS 59. **SS 61:** PU 9 (10, 11) sts on next 9 (10, 11) ridges of LS 58, 1 st in corner, and 9 (10, 11) sts on SS 60. **SS 62:** PU 9 (10, 11) sts on next 9 (10, 11) ridges of LS 58, 1 st in corner, and 9 (10, 11) sts on SS 61. **SS 63:** PU 9 (10, 11) sts on next 9 (10, 11) ridges of LS 58, 1 st in corner, and 9 (10, 11) sts on SS 62.

# FINISHING

## Left Front Band

WITH MC and size 7 needles, PU 19 (21, 23) sts on MS 49, PU 45 (50, 55) sts on LS 58, PU 9 (10, 11) sts on SS 63—73 (81, 89) sts. K 1 row in MC, K 2 rows in CC, K 2 rows in MC, K 2 rows in CC, K 1 row in MC. BO loosely in knit on WS.

## Right Front Band

WITH MC and size 7 needles, PU as for left front band, starting at bottom of SS 57. K 1 row in MC, K 2 rows in CC, K 1 row in MC. With MC, place buttonholes as follows on next row: K3, [K2tog, YO, K9 (10, 11)] 3 times, K2tog, YO, K to end. K 2 rows in CC, K 1 row in MC, BO loosely in knit on WS.

## Neck Edge

WITH SIZE 7 needles and MC, PU 5 sts on top of right front band, 9 (10, 11) sts on half square, 9 (10, 11) sts on each small square around neck, 9 (10, 11) sts on half square, 5 sts on top of left front band— 91 (100, 109) sts. K 1 row in MC, K 2 rows in CC, K 1 row in MC. BO loosely in knit on WS.

## Right Armhole Edge

WITH SIZE 7 needles and CC, starting at underarm, PU 8 (9, 10) sts on LS 18; 19 (21, 23) sts on MS 19, 21, 31, 40, and 46; 8 (9, 10) sts on LS 52. Do not join, turn, K 1 row in CC, K 1 row in MC. BO loosely in knit on WS. Weave armhole border tog.

## Left Armhole Edge

WITH SIZE 7 needles and CC, PU 8 (9, 10) sts on LS 58; 19 (21, 23) sts on MS 50, 45, 38, 30, and 28, and 8 (9, 10) sts on LS 17. Do not join, turn, K 1 row in CC, K 1 row in MC, BO loosely in knit on WS. Weave armhole border tog.

## Bottom Band

STARTING AT lower left front with size 7 needles and CC, PU 5 sts on edge of front band, 9 (10, 11) sts on each small square around to right front, and 5 sts on lower right front band. K 1 row in CC, K1 row in MC. BO loosely in knit on WS.

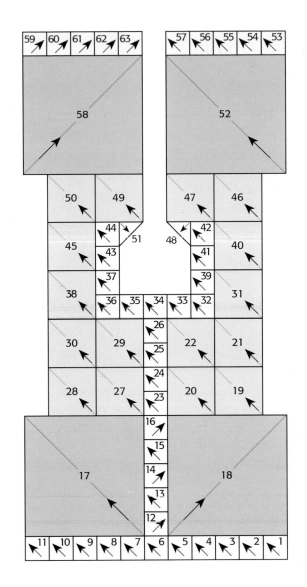

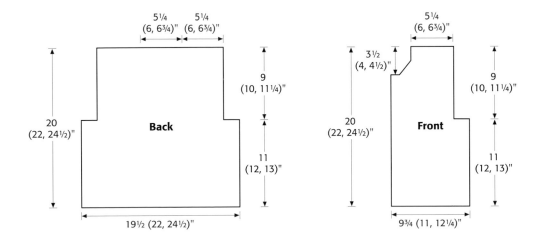

# Shades of Spring Diamonds Vest

*Spring* ◆ *Beginner to Intermediate*

## KNITTED MEASUREMENTS

SIZES: Small (Medium, Large)
FINISHED BUST: 36 (40, 44)"
LENGTH: 19¼ (22, 24)"

## MATERIALS

- 7 (8, 9) skeins of Dolcé by Prism Yarns (70% rayon, 30% nylon, 100yds/50g skein), color 310 or 8 (9, 10) skeins of Bon Bon by Prism Yarns (100% rayon, 94yds/57g skein), color 310 (MC)
- 1 (1, 1½) skeins of Light Stuff by Prism Yarns (mixed fiber content, 400yds/6–7oz skein), Arroyo (CC)
- 2 size 6 circular needles (16" and 29"), or size required to obtain gauge
- About 20 small safety pins
- 5 buttons, ½" to ¾" diameter

NOTE: *Use 2 yarns as listed, or many yarns; you won't be disappointed.*

## GAUGE

1 diamond = 3½ (4, 4⅜)" at the widest point

## PATTERN STITCH FOR GAUGE SWATCH

With MC, CO 25 (29, 33) sts.
**Row 1 (WS):** K12 (14, 16), P1, K12 (14, 16).
**Row 2:** K11 (13, 15), CCD (see page 00), K11 (13, 15).
**Row 3:** K11 (13,15), P1, K11 (13, 15).
**Row 4:** K10 (12,14), CCD, K10 (12, 14).
**Row 5:** K10 (12, 14), P1, K10 (12, 14).
When 11 (13, 15) rows have been completed with the RS facing, change to CC. Cont in this manner, working 1 less st before CCD and purling center on WS rows until 1 st remains. Place this last st on a safety pin.

# Body

With longer size 6 needles and MC, CO 259 (299, 339) sts. K 1 row.

## Beginning Diamonds

This is the first row of diamonds on the chart. *Work across row 2 of "Pattern Stitch for Gauge Swatch" on the first 25 (29, 33) sts only. Cont in patt, change to CC when you have completed 11 (13, 15) rows (as you did for the swatch). Finish diamond. Place last stitch on a pin. Place the next stitch of the CO on a pin and drop off the needle.* Rep from * to * across. Cont in this manner, using all sts that were cast on. You should have 10 diamonds across the bottom with a pin at the top, and 9 sts between the diamonds with pins in them. There should be no stitches left to use, and there will not be a last stitch to place on a pin. Follow the diagram and directions below for placement of the rem diamonds, side half diamonds, and top half diamonds.

Note: *These are garter st diamonds with the center st purled on the WS.*

## Main Diamonds

With RS facing, PU 12 (14, 16) sts on left edge of existing diamond, K the st on the pin, and PU another 12 (14, 16) sts up the right side of the adjoining diamond. Work as you did for gauge swatch starting with row 1; change to CC when you have completed 11 (13, 15) rows. Finish diamond with CC as directed in gauge directions.

## Right Half Diamonds

With RS facing and MC, PU 14 (16, 18) sts, starting at the right lower edge of adjacent diamond. Do not use st on pin of adjacent diamond. **Row 1 (WS):** K12 (14, 16), P1, K1. **Row 2:** K1, SSK, K to end. **Row 3:** K to 2 sts from end, P1, K1. Change to CC when you have completed 11 (13, 15) rows. Cont in this manner, rep rows 2 and 3 until there are 2 sts left. Place on pin.

Note: *On all but the first right half diamond, K across the 2 sts on the pin first, then PU the rem 12 (14, 16) sts, and resume patt.*

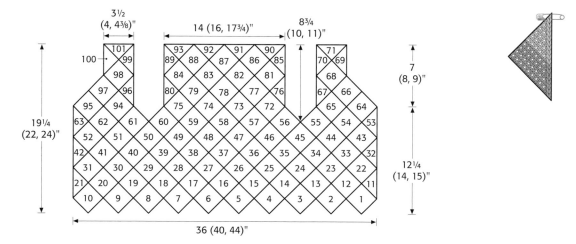

## Left Half Diamond

WITH RS facing and MC, PU 14 (16, 18) sts to the lower front edge. **Row 1:** K1, P1, K to end. **Row 2:** K to 3 sts from end, K2tog, K1. Change to CC when you have completed 11 (13, 15) rows, cont with patt. Rep these 2 rows until there are 2 sts left, place on pin.

NOTE: *On all but the first left half diamond, PU 12 (14, 16) sts, K2 sts from the pin, and then proceed with patt.*

## Top Half Diamond

PU AS for main diamond with MC. Work WS row. On all RS rows, work as given in patt, but work SSK at beg of row and K2tog at end of row. Keep the CCD up the center. On all WS rows, K across, but P the center st. When there are 5 sts left, BO.

# FINISHING

WEAVE TOG shoulder seams.

## Front Band

WITH LONGER size 6 needles and MC, starting at the right lower front, PU 44 (50, 56) sts to start of V neck, 2 sts at V, 36 (42, 48) sts to right shoulder seam, 34 (36, 40) sts across back neck, 36 (42, 48) sts to end of V neck, 2 sts at V, 44 (50, 56) sts to lower left front. K 5 rows. Insert buttonholes on next row. K 4 (5, 6) sts * YO, K2tog, K 7 (8, 9) sts *. Repeat from * to * 4 more times. K to end of row. K 4 more rows. CO 3 st, work 3-st I-cord BO (see page 9).

## Armbands

WITH SHORTER size 6 needles, PU 80 (88, 96) sts as for front, starting at underarm, place marker, and join. P 1 row, K 1 row, P 1 row. CO 3 sts, work 3-st I-cord BO as for front bands.

Weave in all ends. Dampen vest and lay flat, slightly stretching the I-cord border of fronts and armhole. Sew on buttons.

# Thoughts of Spring Diamonds Jacket

*Winter ◆ Intermediate*

## KNITTED MEASUREMENTS

SIZES: Small (Medium, Large, X-Large)
FINISHED BUST: 40 (42½, 44, 46)"
LENGTH: 22 (23, 25, 26)"

## MATERIALS

◆ Great Adirondack Yarns in colorway Speckles
- 2 skeins Twister (100% wool, 300yds/skein) (A)
- 2 skeins Ballerina (100% nylon, 200yds/skein), used double throughout (B)
- 2 skeins Waterfall (39% mohair, 7% wool, 54% nylon, 200yds/skein) (C)
- 2 skeins Persian (36% kid mohair, 62% nylon, 2% polyester, 75yds/skein) (D)
- 1 skein Mikado (96% wool, 4% nylon, 155yds/skein) (E)
◆ Size 9 circular needle (29")
◆ Size 10 circular needle (24"), or size required to obtain gauge
◆ 20 small safety pins
◆ 4 buttons, ¾" diameter

## GAUGE

1 MAIN diamond worked over 19 (21, 23, 25) sts = 4 (4¼, 4⅜, 4¾)" across widest point on size 10 needles

## PATTERN STITCH FOR GAUGE SWATCH

With C and size 10 needles, CO 19 (21, 23, 25) sts.
**Row 1:** P across.
**Row 2:** *K8 (9, 10, 11) sts, work CCD (see page 12), K8 (9, 10, 11) sts.
**Row 3:** P across.*
Rep from * to * working 1 less st before and after dec until 1 st remains. Finish off.

# DIAMOND PATTERNS

SEE PAGE 38 for main-diamond and half-diamond general instructions.

## Main Diamond

PU 9 (10, 11, 12) sts down right side of diamond, K st on pin, PU 9 (10, 11, 12) sts up left side of adjoining diamond—19 (21, 23, 25) sts.

## Right Half Diamond

WITH RS facing, PU 10 (11, 12, 13) sts along right edge of first diamond.

## Left Half Diamond

WITH RS facing, PU 10 (11, 12, 13) sts along the left edge of last diamond.

## Top Half Diamond

PU AS for main diamond.

# BODY

## Border

WITH SIZE 9 needles and A, CO 199 (219, 239, 259) sts. **Row 1 (WS):** [K9 (10, 11, 12) sts, P1] across, end with K9 (10, 11, 12). **Row 2:** K1, M1, K7 (8, 9, 10), work CCD, *K8 (9, 10, 11), M1, K1, M1, K8 (9, 10, 11), work CCD*, rep from * to *, end with K7 (8, 9, 10), M1, K1. Rep rows 1 and 2 three more times. Rep row 1 once.

## Beginning Diamonds

THIS IS the first row of diamonds on the chart. With size 10 needles, working on first 19 (21, 23, 25) sts, K8 (9, 10, 11), work CCD, K8 (9, 10, 11), P back, *K7 (8, 9, 10), work CCD, K7 (8, 9, 10), P back*. Rep from * to *, working 1 less st before and after dec until 1 st remains. Place last st on pin. Cut yarn. Place next st of border on pin. Rep as above for another diamond using appropriate color. Cont in this manner, using all border sts. You should

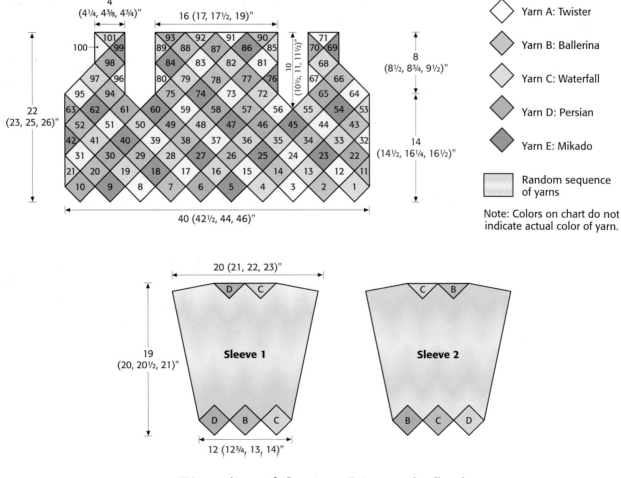

Yarn A: Twister

Yarn B: Ballerina

Yarn C: Waterfall

Yarn D: Persian

Yarn E: Mikado

Random sequence of yarns

Note: Colors on chart do not indicate actual color of yarn.

have 10 diamonds across bottom with a pin at the top and 9 sts between the diamonds with pins in them. There should be no sts left to use, and there will not be a last st to place on a pin. The chart will show you what yarn to use and the order in which to make the diamonds. The next diamond you will work is a right half diamond (11) in B, as shown at the beginning of row 2 on the chart on page 54.

## SLEEVES

### Border

WITH SIZE 9 needles and A, CO 59 (65, 72, 77) sts, work as for border of main body. Change to size 10 needles, work 3 beg diamonds in colors as shown on diagram. There should be 3 diamonds across the bottom with a pin at the top, and 2 sts between the diamonds with pins in them.

### Body

*PU 9 (10, 11, 12) sts up edge of first diamond, K1 st on pin, PU 9 (10, 11, 12) sts down left side of first diamond, K1 st on pin.* Rep from * to * for second and third diamond. **Next row:** *K9 (10, 11, 12), P1*, rep from * to *, end K9 (10, 11, 12).

NOTE: *Use up the remainder of the yarns randomly, working 2, 4, or 6 rows of any given yarn. Yarn sequence in the 2 sleeves should not be the same.*

**Row 1:** K1, SSK, K6 (7, 8, 9), *M1, K1, M1, K8 (9, 10, 11), work CCD, K8 (9, 10, 11)*, rep from * to * twice, M1, K1, M1, K6 (7, 8, 9), K2tog, K1.

NOTE: *Place a pin in the st after the first M1 and before the last M1. Move the pins up as you work to help you keep track of where the increases will be made in row 3.*

**Rows 2 and 4:** P across. **Row 3 (Inc row):** Work as for row 1, but eliminate the dec at beg and end of row 1, making sure to keep track of sts before and after the pins. The number of sts at the beg and the end of row 3 will inc by 1 every time a row 3 is worked. Work rows 1–4 until there are 26 (28, 28, 30) sts before and after the st with the pin. When all increases have been made, work row 1 in place of row 3, working the extra sts into the pattern until sleeve measures 19 (20, 20½, 21)" or desired length. BO all sts, including the st with the first pin. Work top half diamond over next 19 (21, 23, 25) sts. Finish off. Reattach yarn, BO 1 st, work top half diamond over next 19 (21, 23, 25) sts. Finish off. Reattach yarn, BO rem sts.

## FINISHING

WEAVE TOG shoulder seams. Finish off all stitches that remain on pins at top or side edges.

### Front Bands

WITH SIZE 9 needles and RS facing, PU 6 sts along border, PU 10 (11, 12, 13) sts along side of each half diamond to start of V neck, PU 3 sts at point of V, PU 10 (11, 12, 13) sts on edge of each diamond or half diamond around to V neck of left front, PU 3 sts at point of V, PU 10 (11, 12, 13) sts along side of each half diamond to border, PU 6 sts on border of left front, and proceed down left front as for right front, K3 rows. **Buttonhole row:** K2, [K2tog, YO, K8 (9, 10, 11)] 4 times, finish row. Change to size 10 needles, K3 more rows. BO loosely.

Weave sleeves into armholes. Weave in all ends. Steam gently to smooth out diamonds; do not block or steam heavily. The diamonds should have a "puffy" look. Sew on buttons.

# Pinwheel Vest

*Fall* ♦ *Intermediate*

## KNITTED MEASUREMENTS

SIZES: Small (Medium, Large, X-Large)
FINISHED BUST: 38½ (44, 49½, 55)"
LENGTH: 22¾ (26, 29½, 32½)"

## MATERIALS

- 7 (7, 8, 9) skeins of Parfait Swirls by Knit One, Crochet Two (100% wool, 100yds/50g), color 4888 (MC)
- Parfait Solids by Knit One, Crochet Two (100% wool, 210yds/50g)
  - 1 (1, 2, 2) skeins eggplant 1730 (CC1)
  - 1 (1, 2, 2) skeins milk chocolate 1894 (CC2)
  - 1 (1, 2, 2) skeins wine 1292 (CC3)
  - 1 (1, 2, 2) skeins deep evergreen 1565 (CC4)
- Size 8 circular needle (24"), or size required to obtain gauge

- 3 size 8 double-pointed needles
- 2 size 6 double-pointed needles
- 4 buttons, 1" diameter

## GAUGE

1 garter-stitch square worked over 21 (23, 25, 27) sts = 3½ (4, 4½, 5)" on size 8 needles

## GARTER-STITCH SQUARES (GSS)

WORK ALL garter-stitch squares in MC. CO or PU number of sts directed, K back. **Next row (RS):** K9 (10, 11, 12), sl 1, K2tog, psso, K9 (10, 11, 12). K back. *K8 (9, 10, 11), sl 1, K2tog, psso, K8 (9, 10, 11). K back.* Rep from * to *, working 1 less st before and after dec until 1 st remains. Finish off.

# HALF GARTER-STITCH SQUARE (HGSS)

CO or PU number of stitches as directed. K back. SSK, work to center 3 sts, sl 1, K2tog, psso, work to 2 sts from end, K2tog. K back. Rep these 2 rows until there are 3 sts on RS, sl 1, K2tog, psso. Finish off.

# STOCKINETTE-STITCH DIAMONDS (SSD)

WORK ALL stockinette-stitch diamonds in colors CC1, CC2, CC3, or CC4. Use chart to determine which color to use. CO or PU the number of sts as directed, P back. K9 (10, 11, 12), work CCD (see page 12), K9 (10, 11, 12). P back. *K8 (9, 10, 11), work CCD, K8 (9, 10, 11). P bac.* Rep from * to *, working 1 less st before and after dec until 1 st remains. Finish off.

**Notes on reading the chart below:** The arrows show the direction of the knitting and designate the direction of the decreases in the squares. The colors indicate what color yarn to use for each motif. Work each square or diamond as directed; the name of the motif will tell you which direction to follow. You will need to change the direction of the knitting to pick up stitches for some of the motifs.

# LEFT HALF

**SSD 1:** With size 8 circ needles and CC1, CO 21 (23, 25, 27) sts and work SSD. **SSD 2:** With CC2, work as for SSD 1. K tog SSD 1 and 2 and BO as follows: *With size 8 dpn and MC, PU 13, (14, 15, 16) sts along left side of SSD 1. K 1 row. Cut yarn, set aside. With size 8 dpn and MC, PU 13 (14, 15, 16) sts along right side of SSD 1. K 1 row. Do not cut yarn. Holding SSD 1 and SSD 2 with right sides together, work 3-needle BO. Finish off.* (See page 40 for joining SSDs.) **SSD 3:** With CC3, work as for SSD 1. K tog SSD 2 and 3 as described from * to * above. **SSD 4:** With CC4, work as for SSD 1. K tog SSD 3 and 4. K tog SSD 4 and 1.

Weave in all ends. Sew tog center to form pinwheel.

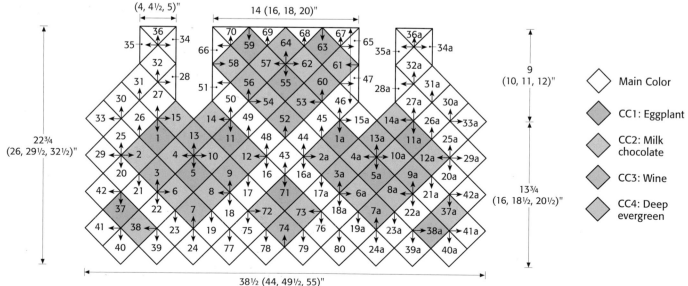

Referring to chart for color and placement, continue on left front as follows:

**SSD 5:** PU 11 (12, 13, 14) sts on SSD 4, CO 10 (11, 12, 13) sts. **SSD 6:** CO 10 (11, 12, 13) sts, PU 11 (12, 13, 14) sts on SSD 3. K tog SSD 5 and 6 as described from * to * in SSD 2. **SSD 7:** CO 21 (23, 25, 27) sts, K tog SSD 6 and 7. **SSD 8:** CO 21 (23, 25, 27) sts. K tog SSD 7 and 8, K tog SSD 8 and 5. **SSD 9:** CO 10 (11, 12, 13) sts, PU 11 (12, 13, 14) sts on SSD 8. **SSD 10:** PU 11 (12, 13, 14) sts on SSD 5, CO 10 (11, 12, 13) sts. K tog SSD 9 and 10. **SSD 11:** CO 21 (23, 25, 27) sts. K tog SSD 10 and 11. **SSD 12:** CO 21 (23, 25, 27) sts. K tog SSD 11 and 12, K tog SSD 12 and 9. **SSD 13:** PU 10 (11, 12, 13) sts on SSD 10, 1 st at point between SSD 10 and 4, and 10 (11, 12, 13) sts on SSD 4. **SSD 14:** CO 10 (11, 12, 13) sts, PU 11 (12, 13, 14) sts on SSD 11. K tog SSD 13 and 14. **SSD 15:** PU 11 (12, 13, 14) sts on SSD 1, CO 10 (11, 12, 13) sts. K tog SSD 13 and 15. **GSS 16:** PU 11 (12, 13, 14) sts on SSD 12, CO 10 (11, 12, 13) sts. **GSS 17:** PU 10 (11, 12, 13) sts on SSD 9, 1 st in corner, and 10 (11, 12, 13) sts on GSS 16. **GSS 18:** PU 10 (11, 12, 13) sts on SSD 8, 1 st in corner, and 10 (11, 12, 13) sts on GSS 17. **GSS 19:** PU 10 (11, 12, 13) sts on SSD 7, 1 st in corner, and 10 (11, 12, 13) sts on GSS 18. **GSS 20:** CO 10 (11, 12, 13) sts, PU 11 (12, 13, 14) sts on SSD 2. **GSS 21:** PU 10 (11, 12, 13) sts on GSS 20, 1 st in corner, and 10 (11, 12, 13) sts on SSD 3. **GSS 22:** PU 10 (11, 12, 13) sts on GSS 21, 1 st in corner, and 10 (11, 12, 13) sts on SSD 6. **GSS 23:** PU 10 (11, 12, 13) sts on GSS 22, 1 st in corner, and 10 (11, 12, 13) sts on SSD 7. **GSS 24:** PU 10 (11, 12, 13) sts on GSS 23, 1 st in corner, and 10 (11, 12, 13) sts on GSS 19. **GSS 25:** PU 11 (12, 13, 14) sts on SSD 2, CO 10 (11, 12, 13) sts. **GSS 26:** PU 10 (11, 12, 13) sts on SSD 1, 1 st in corner, and 10 (11, 12, 13) sts on GSS 25. **GSS 27:** PU 10 (11, 12, 13) sts on SSD 15, 1 st in corner, and 10 (11, 12, 13) sts on GSS 26. **HGSS 28:** PU 10 (11, 12, 13) sts on GSS 27, CO 10 (11, 12, 13) sts. **GSS 29:** PU 10 (11, 12, 13) sts on GSS 25, 1 st in corner, and 10 (11, 12, 13) sts on GSS 20. **GSS 30:** PU 11 (12, 13, 14) sts on GSS 26, CO 10 (11, 12, 13) sts. **GSS 31:** PU 10 (11, 12, 13) sts on GSS 27, 1 st in corner, and 10 (11, 12, 13) sts on GSS 30. **GSS 32:** PU 10 (11, 12, 13) sts on HGSS 28, 1 st in corner, and 10 (11, 12, 13) sts on GSS 31. **GSS 33:** PU 10 (11, 12, 13) sts on GSS 30, 1 st in corner, and 10 (11, 12, 13) sts on GSS 25. **HGSS 34:** PU 11 (12, 13, 14) sts on GSS 32, CO 10 (11, 12, 13) sts. **HGSS 35:** CO 10 (11, 12, 13) sts, PU 11 (12, 13, 14) sts on GSS 32. **HGSS 36:** PU 10 (11, 12, 13) sts on HGSS 34, 1 st in corner, and 10 (11, 12, 13) sts on HGSS 35. **SSD 37:** CO 10 (11, 12, 13) sts, PU 11 (12, 13, 14) sts on GSS 21. **SSD 38:** PU 11 (12, 13, 14) sts on GSS 22, CO 10 (11, 12, 13) sts. K tog SSD 37 and 38 as described for SSD 1 and 2. **GSS 39:** PU 10 (11, 12, 13) sts on SSD 38, 1 st in corner, and 10 (11, 12, 13) sts on GSS 23. **GSS 40:** CO 10 (11, 12, 13) sts, PU 11 (12, 13, 14) sts on SSD 38. **GSS 41:** PU 10 (11, 12, 13) sts on SSD 37, 1 st in corner, and 10 (11, 12, 13) sts on GSS 40. **GSS 42:** PU 10 (11, 12, 13) sts on GSS 20, 1 st in corner, and 10 (11, 12, 13) sts on SSD 37. Set aside.

## RIGHT HALF

WORK SSD 1a–15a as for SSD 1–15 of left front. **GSS 16a:** CO 10 (11, 12, 13) sts, PU 11 (12, 13, 14) sts on SSD 2a. **GSS 17a:** PU 10 (11, 12, 13) sts on GSS 16a, 1 st in corner, and 10 (11, 12, 13) sts on SSD 3a. **GSS 18a:** PU 10 (11, 12, 13) sts on GSS 17a, 1 st in corner, and 10 (11, 12, 13) sts on SSD 6a. **GSS 19a:** PU 10 (11, 12, 13) sts on GSS 18a, 1 st in corner, and 10 (11, 12, 13) sts on SSD 7a. **GSS 20a:** PU 11 (12, 13, 14) sts on SSD 12a, CO 10 (11, 12, 13) sts. **GSS 21a:** PU 10 (11, 12, 13) sts on SSD 9a, 1 st in corner, and 10 (11, 12, 13) sts on GSS 20a. **GSS 22a:** PU 10 (11, 12, 13) sts on SSD 8a, 1 st in corner, and 10 (11, 12, 13) sts on GSS 21a. **GSS 23a:** PU 10 (11, 12, 13) sts on SSD 7a, 1 st in corner, and 10 (11, 12, 13) sts on GSS 22a. **GSS 24a:** PU 10 (11, 12, 13) sts on GSS 19a, 1 st in corner, and 10 (11, 12, 13) sts on GSS 23a. **GSS 25a:** CO 10 (11, 12, 13) sts, PU 11 (12, 13, 14) sts on SSD 12a. **GSS 26a:** PU 10 (11, 12, 13) sts on GSS 25a, 1 st in corner, and 10 (11, 12, 13) sts on SSD 11a. **GSS 27a:** PU 10 (11, 12, 13) sts on GSS 26a,

1 st in corner, and 10 (11, 12, 13) sts on SSD 14a. **HGSS 28a:** CO 10 (11, 12, 13) sts, PU 11 (12, 13, 14) sts on GSS 27a. **GSS 29a:** PU 10 (11, 12, 13) sts on GSS 20a, 1 st in corner, and 10 (11, 12, 13) sts on GSS 25a, work GSS with button loop as follows: Dec until there are 3 sts left. Change to size 6 dpn, work 2½" of I cord (see page 11), or enough I cord to form a loop to accommodate the button you have chosen. Finish off. Make a loop of the I cord and attach to the point of GSS 29a. **GSS 30a:** CO 10 (11, 12, 13) sts, PU 11 (12, 13, 14) sts on GSS 26a. **GSS 31a:** PU 10 (11, 12, 13) sts on GSS 30a, 1 st in corner, and 10 (11, 12, 13) sts on GSS 27a. **GSS 32a:** PU 10 (11, 12, 13) sts on GSS 31a, 1 st in corner, and 10 (11, 12, 13) sts on HGSS 28a. **GSS 33a:** PU 10 (11, 12, 13) sts on GSS 25a, 1 st in corner, and 10 (11, 12, 13) sts on GSS 30a, work GSS with button loop as described for GSS 29a. **HGSS 34a:** PU 11 (12, 13, 14) sts on GSS 32a, CO 10 (11, 12, 13) sts. **HGSS 35a:** CO 10 (11, 12, 13) sts, PU 11 (12, 13, 14) sts on GSS 32a. **HGSS 36a:** PU 10 (11, 12, 13) sts on HGSS 34a, 1 st in corner, and 10 (11, 12, 13) sts on HGSS 35a. **SSD 37a:** PU 11 (12, 13, 14) sts on GSS 21a, CO 10 (11, 12, 13) sts. **SSD 38a:** CO 10 (11, 12, 13) sts, PU 11 (12, 13, 14) sts on GSS 22a, K tog SSD 37a and 38a as described for SSD 1 and 2. **GSS 39a:** PU 10 (11, 12, 13) sts on GSS 23a, 1 st in corner, and 10 (11, 12, 13) sts on SSD 38a. **GSS 40a:** PU 11 (12, 13, 14) sts on SSD 38a, CO 10 (11, 12, 13) sts. **GSS 41a:** PU 10 (11, 12, 13) sts on GSS 40a, 1 st in corner, and 10 (11, 12, 13) sts on SSD 37a, work GSS with button loop as for GSS 29a. **GSS 42a:** PU 10 (11, 12, 13) sts on SSD 37a, 1 st in corner, and 10 (11, 12, 13) sts on GSS 20a, work GSS with button loop as described for GSS 29a.

# JOINING RIGHT AND LEFT FRONT AT CENTER BACK

**GSS 43:** PU 11 (12, 13, 14) sts on GSS 16a, and 10 (11, 12, 13) sts on GSS 16. **GSS 44:** PU 10 (11, 12, 13) sts on SSD 2a, 1 st in corner, and 10 (11, 12, 13) sts on GSS 43. **GSS 45:** PU 10 (11, 12, 13) sts in SSD 1a, 1 st in corner, and 10 (11, 12, 13) sts on GSS 44. **GSS 46:** PU 10 (11, 12, 13) sts on SSD 15a, 1 st in corner, and 10 (11, 12, 13) sts on GSS 45. **HGSS 47:** PU 11 (12, 13, 14) sts on GSS 46, CO 10 (11, 12, 13) sts. **GSS 48:** PU 10 (11, 12, 13) sts on GSS 43, 1 st in corner, and 10 (11, 12, 13) sts on SSD 12. **GSS 49:** PU 10 (11, 12, 13) sts on GSS 48, 1 st in corner, and 10 (11, 12, 13) sts on SSD 11. **GSS 50:** PU 10 (11, 12, 13) sts on GSS 49, 1 st in corner, and 10 (11, 12, 13) sts on SSD 14. **HGSS 51:** CO 10 (11, 12, 13) sts, PU 11 (12, 13, 14) sts on GSS 50. **SSD 52:** PU 10 (11, 12, 13) sts on GSS44, 1 st in corner, and 10 (11, 12, 13) sts on GSS 48. **SSD 53:** CO 10 (11, 12, 13) sts, PU 11 (12, 13, 14) sts on GSS 45. K tog SSD 52 and 53 as described for SSD 1 and 2. **SSD 54:** PU 11 (12, 13, 14) sts on GSS 49, CO 10 (11, 12, 13) sts. K tog SSD 52 and 54. **SSD 55:** CO 21 (23, 25, 27) sts. K tog SSD 54 and 55. K tog SSD 53 and 55. **SSD 56:** PU 10 (11, 12, 13) sts on SSD 54, 1 st in corner, and 10 (11, 12, 13) sts on GSS 50. **SSD 57:** CO 10 (11, 12, 13) sts, PU 11 (12, 13, 14) sts on SSD 55. K tog SSD 56 and 57. **SSD 58:** PU 11 (12, 13, 14) sts on HGSS 51, CO 10 (11, 12, 13) sts. K tog SSD 56 and 58. **SSD 59:** CO 21 (23, 25, 27) sts. K tog SSD 58 and 59. K tog SSD 59 and 57. **SSD 60:** PU 10 (11, 12, 13) sts on GSS 46, 1 st in corner, and 10 (11, 12, 13) sts on SSD 53. **SSD 61:** CO 10 (11, 12, 13) sts, PU 11 (12, 13, 14) sts on HGSS 47. K tog SSD 60 and 61. **SSD 62:** PU 11 (12, 13, 14) sts on SSD 55, CO 10 (11, 12, 13) sts. K tog SSD 60 and 62. **SSD 63:** CO 21 (23, 25, 27) sts. K tog SSD 62 and 63. K tog SSD 63 and 61. **SSD 64:** PU 10 (11, 12, 13) sts on SSD 62, 1 st in corner, and 10 (11, 12, 13) sts on SSD 57. **HGSS 65:** PU 11 (12, 13, 14) sts on SSD 61, CO 10 (11, 12, 13) sts. **HGSS 66:** CO 10 (11,

12, 13) sts, PU 11 (12, 13, 14) sts on SSD 58.
**HGSS 67:** PU 10 (11, 12, 13) sts on HGSS 65, 1 st in corner, and 10 (11, 12, 13) sts on SSD 63. **HGSS 68:** PU 10 (11, 12, 13) sts on SSD 63, 1 st in corner, and 10 (11, 12, 13) sts on SSD 64. **HGSS 69:** PU 10 (11, 12, 13) sts on SSD 64, 1 st in corner, and 10 (11, 12, 13) sts on SSD 59. **HGSS 70:** PU 10 (11, 12, 13) sts on SSD 59, 1 st in corner, and 10 (11, 12, 13) sts on HGSS 66. Turn work so shoulders are down and beg bottom section. **SSD 71:** PU 10 (11, 12, 13) sts on GSS 16, 1 st in corner, and 10 (11, 12, 13) sts on GSS 16a. **SSD 72:** CO 10 (11, 12, 13) sts, PU 11 (12, 13, 14) sts on GSS 17. K tog SSD 71 and 72. **SSD 73:** PU 11 (12, 13, 14) sts on GSS 17a, CO 10 (11, 12, 13) sts, K tog SSD 71 and 73. **SSD 74:** CO 21 (23, 25, 27) sts. K tog SSD 72 and 74. K tog SSD 74 and 73. **GSS 75:** PU 10 (11, 12, 13) sts on GSS 18, 1 st in corner, and 10 (11, 12, 13) sts on SSD 72. **GSS 76:** PU 10 (11, 12, 13) sts on SSD 73, 1 st in corner, and 10 (11, 12, 13) sts on GSS 18a. **GSS 77:** PU 10 (11, 12, 13) sts on GSS 19, 1 st in corner, and 10 (11, 12, 13) sts on GSS 75. **GSS 78:** PU 10 (11, 12, 13) sts on GSS 75, 1 st in corner, and 10 (11, 12, 13) sts on SSD 74. **GSS 79:** PU 10 (11, 12, 13) sts on SSD 74, 1 st in corner, and 10 (11, 12, 13) sts on GSS 76. **GSS 80:** PU 10 (11, 12, 13) sts on GSS 76, 1 st in corner, and 10 (11, 12, 13) sts on GSS 19a. Weave in ends of all GSS on edges of garment; for example, 40, 39, etc.

# FINISHING

## Join Shoulders

WITH SIZE 8 dpn and MC, PU 13, (14, 15, 16) sts across top of right front shoulder, K back. Cut yarn, set aside. Rep for right back shoulder, do not cut yarn, K tog shoulders and BO as you did when joining SSDs. Rep for left front and left back shoulder.

## Armhole Border

WITH SIZE 8 circ needles and MC, starting at bottom of armhole, PU 13 (14, 15, 16) sts on edge of each diamond and half diamond around armhole. Do not join, turn, K 1 row. CO 3 sts and work 3-st I-cord BO (see page 9). When all sts from body are used, graft 3 sts of I cord to CO edge of I cord and finish off. Rep for other armhole.

## Neck Border

WITH SIZE 8 circ needles and MC, start at center left front point next to button loop, PU 11 (12, 13, 14) sts on edge of each diamond, 2 sts on each shoulder around to point of right front. K 1 row. Beg 3-st I-cord BO, using first 3 sts on needle to start. When 2 sts remain on left needle, K1, SSSK, do not turn, K1, SSK. Finish off.

## Optional Front Finishing

IF YOU prefer the center front to be straight on the button edge, work HGSSs in each open triangle area and finish off. You may also apply I cord for a more finished look.

Steam the pinwheels so the centers lie flat. This garment requires a lot of steaming. Sew on buttons.

# Diagonal

THIS HAS BECOME my new favorite technique because the geometry of these garments is like architecture. I can think of no other form of knitting where increases and decreases keep edges straight, where leaving out increases shapes an armhole, or where you can be working on the shoulder shaping and not even be done with the bottom edge yet. Although the directions are a little awkward, the fit and drape are incredible and the knitting is as fun and interesting as it gets. The other terrific part about the whole concept is that all of the edges are in garter stitch, so there is no finishing needed, except for a few seams to sew.

Basically, you begin diagonal knitting in a corner with a few stitches. You work increases at both ends of every row until you achieve the desired width, and then you work decreases at both ends of every row to complete the square or rectangle.

In stockinette stitch, the diagonal-knitting increase and decrease rate presents a problem, because stockinette isn't a "square" stitch. You get more rows to the inch than stitches; the stitch and row gauge usually has about a 3:4 ratio. For example 4 stitches and 6 rows, or 5 stitches and 7 rows, etc. Because of this 3:4 ratio, if you increase at both ends of every row, the piece won't be square; it will grow too quickly at the outside edges and the resulting shape will be more of an elongated diamond. To help keep the knitting square, you need to do the increases and decreases in the same 3:4 ratio as the stitch and row gauge, which means for every 8 rows, you increase 6 times. For example: you would cast on, increase at the beginning and end of the next 3 rows, and skip the increase on the fourth row and then repeat. It is a little crazy to keep track of.

# Knitting

Look at the two examples below, one in stockinette stitch and one in garter stitch. They have exactly the same amount of stitches and rows on the same size needle. Their width is about the same, but the length is considerably longer in the stockinette-stitch sample. When stockinette stitch and garter stitch are combined, the garter stitch is the "controller" for the gauge. This means I was able to use the "square" gauge of garter stitch to work out the increases and decreases for the pattern.

I wanted to create a way to keep track of the increases and decreases without counting out rows on paper or with a row counter. So by combining stockinette-stitch and garter-stitch squares in a grid system drawn on graph paper, I was able to see exactly what was happening and what to do next. Once you understand the grid system, you will need very little written direction.

I worked out an unusual basket-weave stitch in which you knit across the right-side rows and knit 4, purl 4 across the wrong side for a total of 8 rows, and then change to purl 4, knit 4 on the wrong side for 8 rows. You can also knit and purl any other number of stitches—5, 6, or 7, for example—but whatever number you decide on, double it for your row count.

Using the garter-stitch increase ratio, you can work the increases at the beginning and end of every right-side row. It works because the garter-stitch square is the controller and it knits up "square." The borders of the Hemmed Coat with Diagonal Collar and Cuffs is all in garter stitch, so the increases are worked on every other row.

Garter Stitch

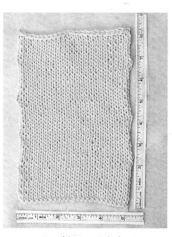

Stockinette Stitch

When developing the pattern, I found that it doesn't matter whether you do the increases one at a time or all at once, and also that you can do something different at each end. So from this came the little points along the bottom edge. Treat those increases as a cast on of 4, or whatever number you are using, and do the increases at the side seam every other row. The end result is the same. Whatever number you choose to make my grid, that is the number of garter-stitch ridges and the number of extra stitches you should have before you move to the next pattern repeat.

I'll use the number 4 to demonstrate the grid system. Knit the following sample to increase your understanding of this technique.

CO 1 more stitch than the number you chose for your pattern (in our case, 5).

**Row 1 (WS):** K4, P1. Turn, look at RS; you have 1 garter-stitch ridge and 1 extra st at the right edge.

**Row 2 and all even rows:** K1, M1, K to the end.

NOTE: You must use M1 inc for this st pattern to work.

**Row 3:** K4, P2. 2 garter-stitch ridges and 2 extra sts on RS.

**Row 5:** K4, P3. 3 garter-stitch ridges and 3 extra sts on RS.

**Row 7:** K4, P4. 4 garter-stitch ridges and 4 extra sts on RS. Go to next row of squares on chart.

**Row 9:** CO 4 sts, K4, P4, K4, P1.

**Row 11:** K4, P4, K4, P2.

**Row 13:** K4, P4, K4, P3.

**Row 15:** (K4, P4) twice. Go to next row of squares on chart.

**Row 17:** CO 4 sts (K4, P4) twice, K4, P1.

**Row 19:** (K4, P4) twice, K4, P2.

**Row 21:** (K4, P4) twice, K4, P3.

**Row 23:** (K4, P4) 3 times.

Look at the sample of knitting and the grid at right that matches it. You can see they match exactly. Each green square represents a garter-stitch square and each white square a stockinette-stitch square. You don't go to the next row of squares on the chart until you have completed the number of rows required for the section. The same chart will work for any multiple of stitches with adjustments for length and width.

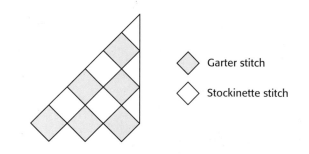

Garter stitch

Stockinette stitch

You do have to keep your wits about you with these sweaters because in some patterns you might be starting the right armhole before you reach the full width of the bottom edge. You probably won't work the left armhole until you've started shaping the top edge. This is absolutely intriguing to my mind. To help keep track of your position on the chart, mark off the sections as you complete them.

# Diagonal-Knit Purse

## KNITTED MEASUREMENTS

10" wide x 10" high x 1" deep

## MATERIALS

- 2 skeins Cascade 220 by Cascade Yarns (100% wool, 220yds/100g), color 9484
- Sizes 5 and 8 needles, or size required to obtain gauge
- 1 yd. of 1"-wide heavy webbing for handle
- 2 ring markers
- 2 safety pins
- ½ yd. fabric for lining
- 1 yd. Pellon Craft-Fuse
- 1 button, 1" diameter

## GAUGE

16 sts and 24 rows = 4" in pattern stitch on size 8 needles

## Pattern Stitch for Gauge Swatch

*(Multiple of 8 sts and 8 rows)*
CO 24 sts.
**Row 1 and all odd rows:** K across.
**Rows 2 and 4:** K4, P4.
**Rows 6 and 8:** P4, K4.

## Back

With size 8 needles, CO 42 sts.
*****Row 1:** K across.
**Row 2:** K1 (K4, P4) across, end K1.
Rep rows 1 and 2 three more times.
**Row 3:** K across.
**Row 4:** K1 (P4, K4) across, end K1.
Rep rows 3 and 4 three more times*.
Rep from * to * 4 more times. BO. This is the top edge.
Trace the shape on a piece of paper to use as a lining pattern later.

## Gusset

Hold back with RS facing. With size 8 needles, PU 42 sts down left edge, PM, PU 42 sts across bottom , PM, and 42 sts up right edge—126 sts.
**Rows 1 and 4:** (K2, P2) to last 2 sts, end K2.
**Rows 2 and 3:** (P2, K2) to last 2 sts, end P2.
Rep rows 1 and 2 one more time. BO loosely, replacing markers with safety pins to designate corners.
Measure length and width of gusset and make a paper pattern to use as a lining pattern later.

## Front (in 4 Sections)

### Section 1

On gusset right edge with RS facing, and size 8 needles, PU 38 sts to corner, or where safety pin is located.
**Row 1 (WS):** K across.
**Row 2 and all even-numbered rows not listed:** K1, SSK, K to last 3 sts, K2tog, K1.
**Row 3:** K4, (P4, K4) to end.
**Row 5:** K3, (P4, K4) to last 7 sts, P4, K3.
**Row 7:** K2, (P4, K4) to last 6 sts, P4, K2.
**Row 9:** K5, (P4, K4) to last 9 sts, P4, K5.
**Row 11:** K4, (P4, K4) to end.
**Row 13:** K3, (P4, K4) to last 7 sts, P4, K3.
**Row 15:** K2, (P4, K4) to last 6 sts, P4, K2.
**Row 17:** K5, (P4, K4) to last 9 sts, P4, K5.
**Row 19:** K4, (P4, K4) to end.
**Row 21:** K3, (P4, K4) to last 7 sts, P4, K3.
**Row 23:** K2, P4, K4, P4, K2.
**Row 25:** K5, P4, K5.
**Row 27:** K4, P4, K4.
**Row 29:** K3, P4, K3.
**Row 31:** K2, P4, K2.
**Row 33:** K across.
**Row 35:** K across.
**Row 36:** K1, SSK, K1.
**Row 37:** K across.
**Row 38:** Sl 1, K2tog, psso. Finish off.

### Section 2

Rep directions for section 1 to second pin.

## Section 3

REP DIRECTIONS for section 1 to top edge.

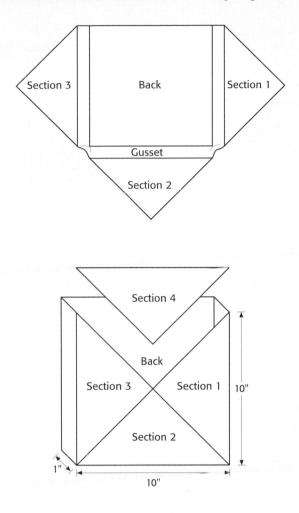

**Section 4:** With size 8 needles, CO 38 sts, K 2 rows. Work rows 1–38 as for section 1. Weave tog sections 1–3, and then weave section 4 into the empty space to create a square front.

## FLAP

WITH SIZE 8 needles, CO 12 sts, K across. K 6 more rows.

**Rows 1, 9, 17, 25 (RS):** CO 4 sts, K across.

**Rows 2, 4, 6, 8:** K8, P4, K4.

**Row 3 and all odd rows not listed (RS):** K across.

**Rows 10, 12, 14, 16:** K12, P4, K4.

**Rows 18, 20, 22, 24:** K8, (P4, K4) twice.

**Rows 26, 28, 30, 32:** K12, (P4, K4) twice.

**Row 29 (buttonhole row):** K2, YO, SSK, K
    to end.

**Rows 33, 41, 49, 57:** BO 4 sts, K across.

**Rows 34, 36, 38, 40:** K8, (P4, K4) twice.

**Rows 42, 44, 46, 48:** K12, P4, K4.

**Rows 50, 52, 54, 56:** K8, P4, K4.

**Row 57:** BO 4 sts. K across.

K 6 more rows. BO all sts.

Sew to top of back side of purse, easing to fit across.

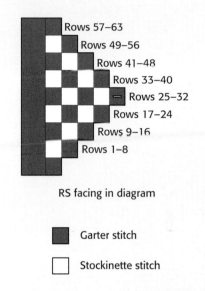

RS facing in diagram

■ Garter stitch

□ Stockinette stitch

## HANDLE

HOLD GUSSET on left side of purse with RS facing. With size 5 needles, CO 4 sts, PU 8 sts across gusset, CO 4 more sts using cable CO—16 sts. **Row 1:** K4, sl 1 wyif, K6, sl 1 wyif, K4. **Row 2:** K across. Rep these 2 rows until handle measures 26", ending with row 1. BO all sts. Sew to right side of gusset. Steam gently before lining.

**Handle finishing:** Cut webbing slightly longer than handle. Attach at both ends of gusset. Fold handle at slipped stitches and weave seam together covering webbing on underside of handles.

See "Lining Purses" (page 124) for lining instructions. The flap is not lined.

# Hemmed Coat with Diagonal Collar and Cuffs

*Fall ◆ Beginner*

## KNITTED MEASUREMENTS

SIZES: Small (Medium, Large, X-Large)
FINISHED BUST: 40 (44, 48, 52)"
LENGTH: 24¼ (26½, 27¼, 27¾)"

## MATERIALS

- 5 (6, 6, 7) skeins 4/8 Wool by Mountain Colors (100% wool, 250yds/114g), Rich Red (MC)
- 1 (2, 2, 2) skeins Merino Ribbon by Mountain Colors (80% superfine merino wool, 20% nylon, 245yds/114g), Sunrise (CC)
- Sizes 5, 7, and 8 needles, or size required to obtain gauge
- 6 stitch holders
- 2 buttons, 1" diameter

## GAUGE

**For MC:** 20 sts and 28 rows = 4" in stockinette stitch on size 7 needles
**For CC:** 16 sts and 32 rows = 4" in garter stitch on size 8 needles

# BACK

WITH SIZE 5 needles and MC, use provisional CO (see page 7) to CO 104 (112, 122, 132) sts. *Work St st for 8 rows for hem, change to size 8 needles, work 8 more rows. Remove provisional CO, placing hem sts on size 5 needle, K the hem and the body sts tog (see page 8). Cont in St st on size 8 needles until piece measures 3" from beg, end with a P row.* Beg side shaping as follows: Dec 1 st each end now and every 8 (14, 12, 14) rows 3 (2, 5, 3) times, then dec 1 st each end every 6 (12, 0, 12) rows 2 (3, 0, 2) times—92 (100, 110, 120) sts. Cont in St st until piece measures 11 (12, 12½, 13½)". Cont side shaping as follows: Inc 1 st at each end now and every 6 (6, 4, 4) rows 5 (4, 2, 3) times, then inc 1 st at each end every 0 (8, 6, 6) rows 0 (1, 3, 2) times—104 (112, 122, 132) sts. Work even in St st until piece measures 16 (18, 18, 18¼)", end with a P row.

**Beg armhole shaping:** BO 5 (5, 5, 5,) sts at beg of next 2 rows. Dec 1 st each end EOR 9 (13, 16, 18) times—76 (76, 80, 86) sts. Work even in St st until armhole measures 8¼ (8¼, 9¼, 9½)", end with a P row.

**Shoulder shaping:** Work across 27 (27, 28, 31) sts, BO center 22 (22, 24, 24) sts, work across. Work each shoulder separately or use a second ball of yarn and work both shoulders at the same time.

**Shoulder and neck shaping:** At neck edge dec 1 st EOR 4 (4, 4, 4) times, and at the same time work short-row shoulder shaping as follows (see page 94): For right front and left back, K across to last 4 (4, 5, 5) sts, W and T, P back. (K across to 5 (5, 5, 6) sts from last W and T, turn, P back) 3 (3, 3, 2) times. K across row, knitting up wraps. For right back and left front, on the next WS row, P across to last 4 (4, 4, 5) sts, W and T, K back. (P across to 5 (5, 5, 6) sts from last W and T, K back) 3 (3, 3, 2) times. P across row purling up wraps.

# LEFT FRONT

WITH SIZE 5 needles and MC, use provisional CO to CO 53 (56, 61, 66) sts. Work as for back from * to *.

**Beg side shaping:** Dec 1 st at beg of row now and every 8 (14, 12, 14) rows 3 (2, 5, 3) times, then dec 1 st at beg of row every 6 (12, 0, 12) rows 2 (3, 0, 2) times—47 (50, 55, 60) sts. Cont in St st until piece measures 11 (12, 12½, 13½)". Cont side shaping: Inc 1 st at beg of row now and every 6 (6, 4, 4) rows 5 (4, 2, 3) times, then inc 1 st at beg of row every 0 (8, 6, 6) rows 0 (1, 3, 2) times—53 (56, 61, 66) sts. Work even in St st until piece measures 16 (18, 18, 18¼)", end with a P row.

**Beg armhole and neck shaping:** At armhole edge, BO 5 (5, 5, 5) sts at beg of next row, dec 1 st EOR 9 (13, 16, 18) times. At the same time at neck edge: dec 1 st now and every 4 (4, 4, 4) rows 13 (10, 10, 7) times, then dec 1 st every 6 (6, 6, 6) rows 2 (4, 5, 8) times—23 (23, 24, 27) sts. When armhole measures 8¼ (8¼, 9¼, 9½)", work shoulder shaping as for back at armhole edge: leave 4 (4, 4, 5) sts once, leave 5 (5, 5, 6) sts 3 (3, 4, 2) times, leave 4 (4, 0, 5) sts 1 (1, 0, 2) times. K or P the next row to pick up the wraps. Place shoulder sts on holders.

# RIGHT FRONT

WORK AS for left front, reversing shaping.

# RIGHT SLEEVE CUFF

*WITH SIZE 8 needles and CC, CO 3 sts. K across. **Row 1 (RS):** K1, M1, K1, M1, K1. **Row 2:** K across. **Row 3:** K1, M1, K3, M1, K1. **Row 4:** K across. **Row 5:** K1, M1, K5, M1, K1. **Row 6:** K across. Cont in this manner, working M1 at beg and end of row until there are 35 sts, end with a RS row.* **Next row and all WS rows:** K to last 3 sts, sl 3 sts wyib. **Next row and all RS rows:** K2, SSK, K to last st, M1, K1. Rep these 2 rows until long edge measures 11½ (11½, 12, 12½)", end with a WS row. **Next row and all RS rows:** K2, SSK, K to last 2 sts, K2tog. **WS rows:** K to last 3 sts, sl 3 wyif. Work the last 2 rows until 5 sts remain. On next RS row, K2, sl 1 wyib, K2tog, psso. BO 3 sts.

## LEFT SLEEVE CUFF

WORK AS for right sleeve cuff from * to *. **Next row and all WS rows:** Sl 3 sts wyif, K across. **Next row and all RS rows:** K1, M1, K to last 4 sts, K2tog, K2. When long edge measures 11½ (11½, 12, 12½)", end with a WS row. **Next row and all RS rows:** SSK, K to last 4 sts, K2tog, K2. **Next row and all WS rows:** Sl 3 sts wyif, K across. Work the last 2 rows until 5 sts remain. On next RS row, K2, sl 1, K2tog, psso. BO 3 sts. Mark cuffs with notes to designate right and left.

## SLEEVES (MAKE 2)

WITH SIZE 8 needles and MC, PU 46 (50, 50, 52) sts with WS of cuff facing. Work 2 rows in St st. **Beg sleeve shaping:** Inc 1 st at each end now and every 6 (6, 5, 5) rows 5 (6, 8, 4) times, then inc 1 st at each end every 7 (8, 6, 6) rows 10 (8, 9, 13) times—78 (80, 86, 88) sts. Work even until sleeve measures 14 (14½, 15, 16)" from picked-up edge of cuff. **Beg armhole shaping:** BO 5 (5, 5, 5) sts at beg of next 2 rows, dec 1 st at each end EOR 16 (21, 22, 26) times, dec 1 st at each end every row 10 (5, 6, 3) times. BO rem 16 (18, 20, 20) sts.

## LEFT FRONT BORDER

WORK AS for right sleeve cuff from * to * until there are 29 sts. End with RS row. **Next row and all WS rows:** K to last 3 sts, sl 3 sts wyib. **Next row and all RS rows:** K2, SSK, K to last st, M1, K1. Work the last 2 rows until long edge of piece reaches to center back neck slightly stretched, end with WS row. NOTE: *There are no more increases or decreases.* Beg short-row shaping for back neck *Next 2 rows: K to last 2 sts, W and T (see page 93), K to last 3 sts, sl 3 wyif. Proceed in this manner, working short rows 2 sts less from previous W and T, K to last 3 sts, sl 3 wyif. End with WS row

with only the 3 sts to be slipped on WS row, K across on RS, turn, K to last 3 sts, sl 3 wyif.* Rep from * to *, working to 4 sts from end instead of 2 sts, W and T, K to last 3 sts, sl 3 wyif. Cont working short rows every 4 sts. When there are only the 3 sts to be slipped on WS row, K across on RS, knitting up wraps. Next row: K to last 3 sts, sl 3 wyif. Place sts on holder.

## RIGHT FRONT BORDER

WORK AS for right sleeve cuff from * to * until there are 29 sts. End with RS row. **Next row and all WS rows:** Sl 3 sts wyif, K across. **Next row and all RS rows:** K1, M1, K to last 4 sts, K2tog, K2. Work these 2 rows until long edge of piece measures same as left front border to back neck shaping, end with RS row. NOTE: *There are no more increases or decreases.* Beg short-row shaping on WS rows *Next 2 rows: Sl 3 sts wyif, K to last 2 sts, W and T, K across. Proceed in this manner, working short rows 2 sts less from previous W and T, K across. End with RS row and when there are only the 3 sts to be slipped on WS row, sl 3 sts wyif, K across, knitting up wraps.* Turn, K 1 row. Rep from * to *, working to last 4 sts instead of 2 sts, W and T, K across. Cont working short rows every 4 sts. Cont until there are only the 3 sts to be slipped on the WS row. Sl 3 sts wyif, K across, knitting up wraps, place sts on holder. Graft tog left and right front borders (see page 8).

## FINISHING

JOIN SHOULDERS with 3-needle BO (see page 10). Mark placement for 2 buttons on left front, one directly below beg of V neck and another 2½ (3, 3, 3½)" below.

With size 5 needles, and MC, CO 3 sts. Work I-cord for 3" (see page 11). Fold in half to make a button loop and attach to right front across from button placement. Repeat for second button loop.

Weave border to right front edge with WS of border and RS of coat facing. Weave border to left front edge with WS of border and RS of coat facing, leaving 1" unattached where button will be sewn on.

With size 7 needles and MC, CO 3 sts, work attached I cord (see page 10) to 3 out of every 4 rows, starting at lower right front seam, where border is sewn to front of coat, and ending at lower left front. Finish off.

Weave sleeves into armholes. Be sure left and right sleeves go in appropriate armhole. Weave sleeve and side seams. Weave tog cuff seam with RS facing, so seam is against sleeve when cuff is folded up.

Tack collar to shoulder seams and to center front. Steam gently.

NOTE: *The hem may require more steaming to make it lie flat.*

Sew on buttons under left lapel across from buttonholes, far enough away from the edge so that the two fronts meet exactly.

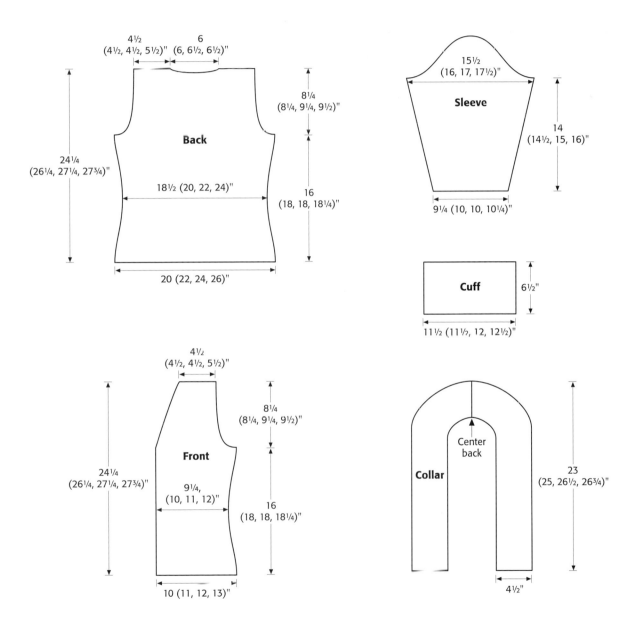

**Back**

4½
(4½, 4½, 5½)"

6
(6, 6½, 6½)"

8¼
(8¼, 9¼, 9½)"

24¼
(26¼, 27¼, 27¾)"

18½ (20, 22, 24)"

16
(18, 18, 18¼)"

20 (22, 24, 26)"

**Sleeve**

15½
(16, 17, 17½)"

14
(14½, 15, 16)"

9¼ (10, 10, 10¼)"

**Cuff**

6½"

11½ (11½, 12, 12½)"

**Front**

4½
(4½, 4½, 5½)"

8¼
(8¼, 9¼, 9½)"

24¼
(26¼, 27¼, 27¾)"

9¼,
(10, 11, 12)"

16
(18, 18, 18¼)"

10 (11, 12, 13)"

**Collar**

Center
back

23
(25, 26½, 26¾)"

4½"

# Diagonal-Knit Vest

## KNITTED MEASUREMENTS

SIZES: Small (Medium, Large)
FINISHED BUST: 40 (44, 48)"
LENGTH: 22 (22, 26)"

## MATERIALS

◆ 3 (4, 6) skeins Magpie Tweed by Rowan
  (100% wool, 185yds/100g), color 775
◆ Size 8 circular needle (29"), or size required to
  obtain gauge
◆ 3 (3, 4) buttons, 1" diameter

## GAUGE

16 sts and 24 rows = 4" in pattern stitch

## PATTERN STITCH FOR GAUGE SWATCH

*(Multiple of 8 sts and 16 rows)*
CO 32 sts.
**Rows 1, 3, 5, 7 (WS):** (K4, P4) across.
**Rows 2 and all even-numbered rows:** K across.
**Rows 9, 11, 13, 15:** (P4, K4) across.
Rep these 16 rows.

## Back and Left Front

Follow chart for your size to work back and fronts. The chart shows whether a square is garter stitch or stockinette stitch with the RS facing you. Mark off the sections as you complete them. The first two sections are outlined below so that you can see how the pattern works.

**All sizes:**
CO 5 sts.
**Row 1 (WS):** K4, P1.
**Row 2 and all even-numbered rows:** K1, M1, K across.
**Row 3:** K4, P2.
**Row 5:** K4, P3.
**Row 7:** K4, P4
From this point, each section has 8 rows. At the end of 8 rows, you should have 4 garter-stitch ridges in each garter-stitch section.
**Row 9:** CO 4 sts, K4, P4, K4, P1.
**Row 11:** K4, P4, K4, P2.
**Row 13:** K4, P4, K4, P3.
**Row 15:** (K4, P4) twice.
Cont with appropriate chart for your size, working inc and dec into patt on WS.

## Right Front

**All sizes:**
CO 5 sts.
**Row 1 (WS):** P1, K4.
**Row 2 and all even-numbered rows (unless listed):** K to 1 st from end, M1, K1.
**Row 3:** P2, K4.
**Row 5:** P3, K4.
**Row 7:** P4, K4.
From this point, each section has 8 rows. At the end of 8 rows, you should have 4 garter-stitch ridges in each garter-stitch section.
**Row 8:** CO 4 sts, K to 1 st from end, M1, K1.
**Row 9:** P1, K4, P4, K4.
**Row 11:** P2, K4, P4, K4.
**Row 13:** P3, K4, P4, K4.
**Row 15:** (P4, K4) twice.
Cont with appropriate chart for your size, working inc and dec into patt on WS.

Work buttonholes on the following rows:

### Small

**Rows 68, 84, 100:** K1, K2tog, YO, finish row per chart.

### Medium

**Rows 76, 92, 108:** K1, K2tog, YO, finish row per chart.

### Large

**Rows 92, 108, 124, 140:** K1, K2tog, YO, finish row per chart.

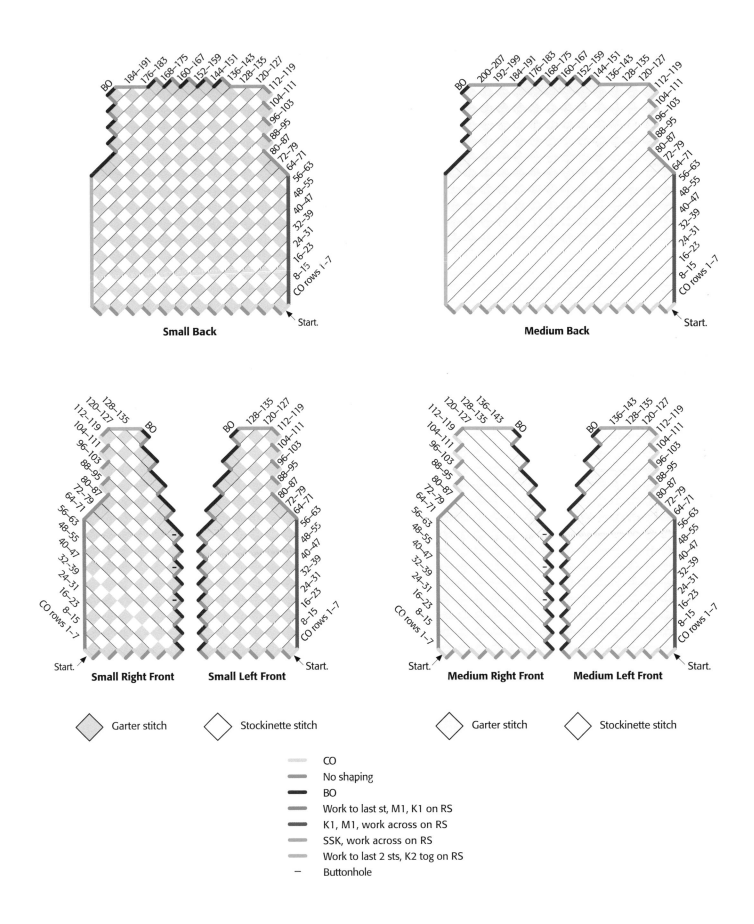

**Small Back**

**Medium Back**

**Small Right Front**

**Small Left Front**

**Medium Right Front**

**Medium Left Front**

◇ Garter stitch  ◇ Stockinette stitch

◇ Garter stitch  ◇ Stockinette stitch

CO

No shaping

BO

Work to last st, M1, K1 on RS

K1, M1, work across on RS

SSK, work across on RS

Work to last 2 sts, K2 tog on RS

− Buttonhole

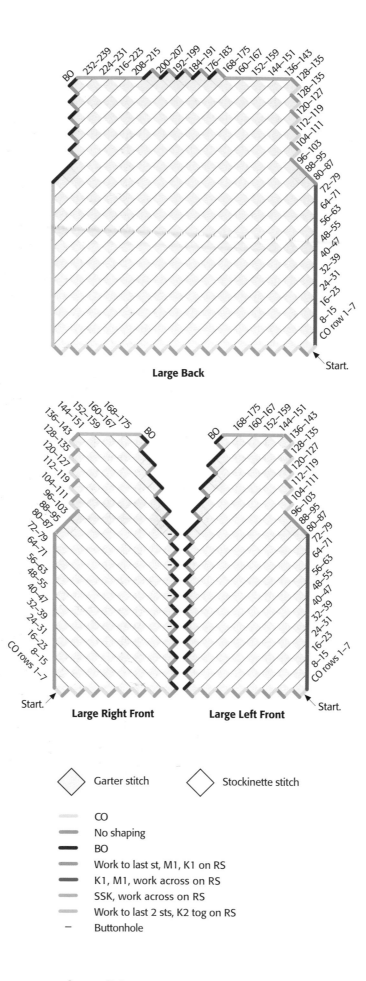

**Large Back**

**Large Right Front**          **Large Left Front**

◇ Garter stitch          ◇ Stockinette stitch

CO

No shaping

BO

Work to last st, M1, K1 on RS

K1, M1, work across on RS

SSK, work across on RS

Work to last 2 sts, K2 tog on RS

− Buttonhole

# FINISHING

WEAVE TOG shoulder seams. Lay flat, spray with water, pin out each point and leave flat until dry. Be sure side seams are same length. Remove pins, weave side seams, gently steam the side seams. Sew on buttons.

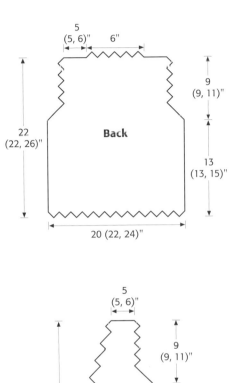

# Diagonal-Knit Coat with Diagonal Collar and Cuffs

*Winter* ◆ *Intermediate*

## KNITTED MEASUREMENTS

SIZES: Small (Medium, Large)
FINISHED BUST: 42 (46, 52)"
LENGTH: 22 (26, 28)"

## MATERIALS

- 7 (8, 10) skeins Donegal Tweed by Tahki (100% wool, 183 yds/100g), color 853
- Sizes 7 and 9 needles, or size required to obtain gauge
- 5 (5, 6) buttons, 1" diameter

## GAUGE

14 sts and 24 rows = 4" in pattern stitch on size 9 needles

## PATTERN STITCH FOR GAUGE SWATCH AND SLEEVES

*(Multiple of 10 sts and 20 rows)*
CO 40 sts.
**Rows 1, 3, 5, 7, 9 (WS):** (K5, P5) across.
**Row 2 and all even-numbered rows:** K across.
**Rows 11, 13, 15, 17, 19:** (P5, K5) across.
Rep these 20 rows.

## BACK AND LEFT FRONT

FOLLOW CHART for your size to work back and left front. The chart shows whether a square is garter stitch or stockinette stitch with the RS facing you. Mark off the sections as you complete them. I have outlined the first 2 sections below so that you can see how the pattern works.

**All sizes:**

With size 9 needles, CO 6 sts.

**Row 1 (WS):** K5, P1.

**Row 2 and all even-numbered rows:** K1, M1, K to end.

**Row 3:** K5, P2.

**Row 5:** K5, P3.

**Row 7:** K5, P4.

**Row 9:** K5, P5.

From this point, each section has 10 rows. At the end of the 10 rows, you should have 5 garter-stitch ridges in each garter-stitch section.

**Row 11:** CO 5 sts, K5, P5, K5, P1.

**Row 13:** K5, P5, K5, P2

**Row 15:** K5, P5, K5, P3.

**Row 17:** K5, P5, K5, P4

**Row 19:** (K5, P5) twice.

Cont with appropriate chart for your size, working inc and dec into patt on WS.

# RIGHT FRONT

**All sizes:**

With size 9 needles, CO 6 sts.

**Row 1 (WS):** P1, K5.

**Row 2 and all even-numbered rows without cast on:** K to 1 st from end, M1, K1.

**Row 3:** P2, K5.

**Row 5:** P3, K5.

**Row 7:** P4, K5.

**Row 9:** P5, K5.

From this point, each section has 10 rows. At the end of the 10 rows, you should have 5 garter-stitch ridges in each garter-stitch section.

**Row 10:** CO 5 sts, K to 1 st from end, M1, K1.

**Row 11:** P1, K5, P5, K5.

**Row 13:** P2, K5, P5, K5.

**Row 15:** P3, K5, P5, K5.

**Row 17:** P4, K5, P5, K5

**Row 19:** (P4, K5) twice.

Cont with appropriate chart for your size, working inc and dec into patt on WS.

Work buttonholes on the following rows:

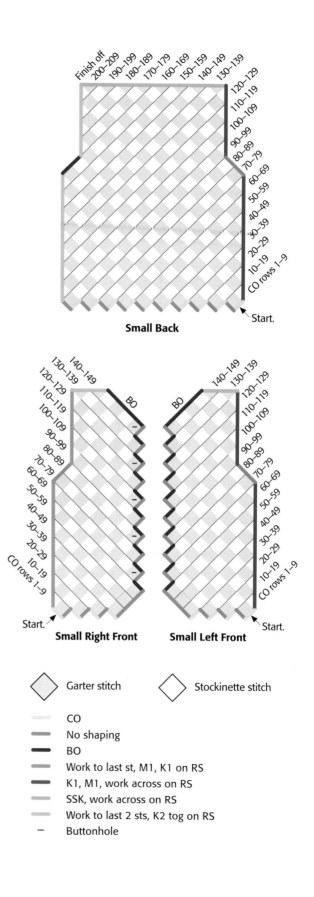

**Small Back**

**Small Right Front**   **Small Left Front**

◇ Garter stitch   ◇ Stockinette stitch

— CO
— No shaping
— BO
— Work to last st, M1, K1 on RS
— K1, M1, work across on RS
— SSK, work across on RS
— Work to last 2 sts, K2 tog on RS
– Buttonhole

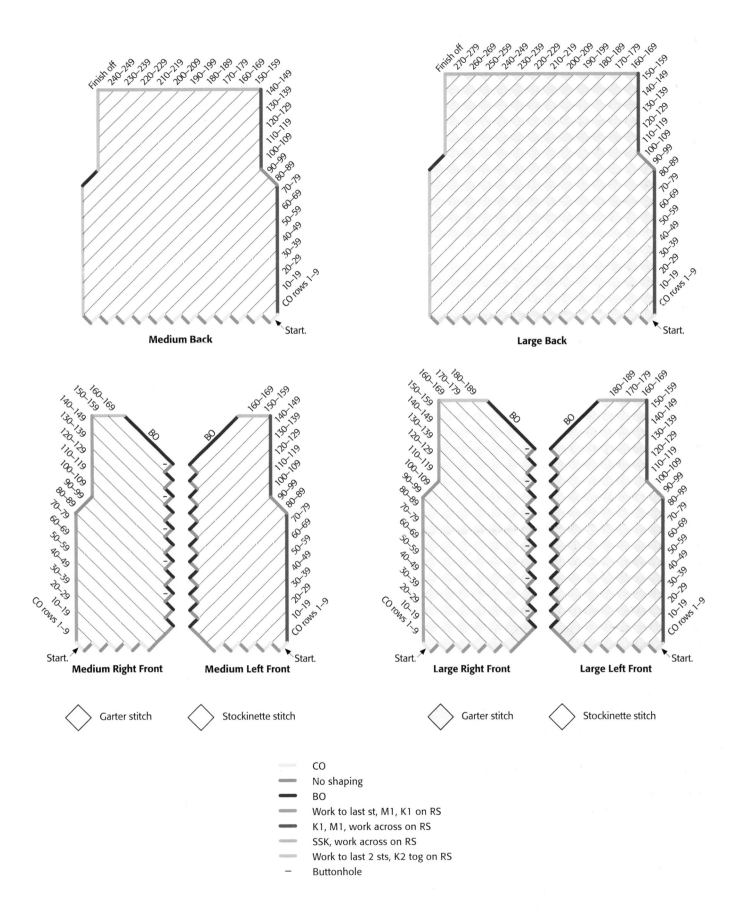

**Medium Back**

**Large Back**

**Medium Right Front**     **Medium Left Front**

**Large Right Front**     **Large Left Front**

◇ Garter stitch      ◇ Stockinette stitch

◇ Garter stitch      ◇ Stockinette stitch

CO

No shaping

BO

Work to last st, M1, K1 on RS

K1, M1, work across on RS

SSK, work across on RS

Work to last 2 sts, K2 tog on RS

– Buttonhole

## Small

**Row 65:** P3 (K5, P5) 4 times, K1, YO, K2tog, K2.

**Row 85:** (P5, K5) 3 times, P5, K1, YO, K2tog, K2.

**Rows 105, 125:** P3, (K5, P5) 3 times, K1, YO, K2tog, K2. Rep once.

**Row 145:** K2, P5, K5, P5, K1, YO, K2tog, K2.

## Medium

**Row 85:** (K5, P5) 5 times, K1, YO, K2tog, K2.

**Rows 105, 125, 145:** P3, (K5, P5) 4 times, K1, YO, K2tog, K2. Rep twice.

**Row 165:** K2, (P5, K5) 2 times, P5, K1, YO, K2tog, K2.

## Large

**Row 85:** P3, (K5, P5) 6 times, K1, YO, K2tog, K2.

**Row 105:** (P5, K5), 5 times, P5, K1, YO, K2tog, K2.

**Rows 125, 145:** P3, (K5, P5) 5 times, K1, YO, K2tog, K2.

**Row 165:** K2, (P5, K5) 4 times, P5, K1, YO, K2tog, K2.

**Row 185:** K2, (P5, K5) 2 times, P5, K1, YO, K2tog, K2.

# SLEEVES (MAKE 2)

**For all sizes:**
**Cuff:** With size 9 needles, CO 6 sts.
**Row 1 (WS):** K5, P1.
Proceed with chart as for back.

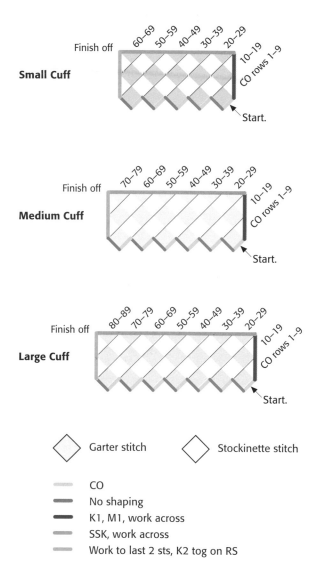

With WS of cuff facing, PU 30 (40, 40) sts. K across, inc 2 (2, 2) sts evenly across. K 2 more rows. Beg pattern stitch for gauge swatch and sleeves, leaving 1 st on each edge in St st for seam. Inc 1 st at each end on row 5 and every 4 rows 17 (15, 15) times. When sleeve measures 16 (17, 18)" or desired length, BO.

# COLLAR

BEGIN AS for cuff, following chart for appropriate size.

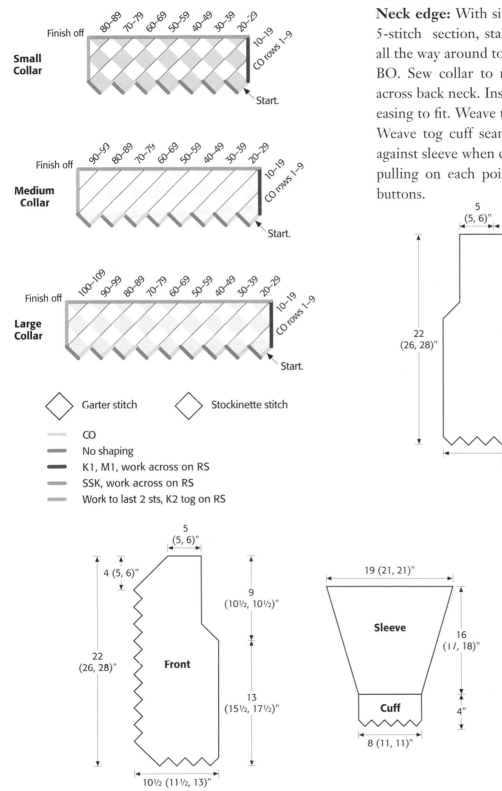

**Small Collar**

Finish off

80–89 70–79 60–69 50–59 40–49 30–39 20–29

10–19

CO rows 1–9

Start.

**Medium Collar**

Finish off

90–99 80–89 70–79 60–69 50–59 40–49 30–39 20–29

10–19

CO rows 1–9

Start.

**Large Collar**

Finish off

100–109 90–99 80–89 70–79 60–69 50–59 40–49 30–39 20–29

10–19

CO rows 1–9

Start.

◇ Garter stitch    ◇ Stockinette stitch

— CO
— No shaping
— K1, M1, work across on RS
— SSK, work across on RS
— Work to last 2 sts, K2 tog on RS

# FINISHING

WEAVE TOG shoulder seams. Lay flat, spray with water, pin out each point and leave flat until dry. Be sure side seams are same length. Remove pins. **Neck edge:** With size 7 needles, PU 4 sts in each 5-stitch section, starting at right front neck edge all the way around to left front neck edge. K 1 row. BO. Sew collar to neck edge, stretching slightly across back neck. Insert sleeve into sleeve opening, easing to fit. Weave tog side seam and sleeve seam. Weave tog cuff seam with RS facing, so seam is against sleeve when cuff is folded up. Steam gently, pulling on each point; lay flat until dry. Sew on buttons.

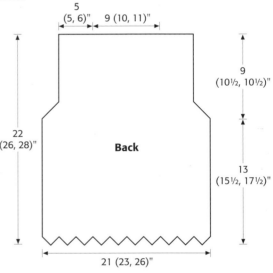

5
(5, 6)"    9 (10, 11)"

9
(10½, 10½)"

22
(26, 28)"

**Back**

13
(15½, 17½)"

21 (23, 26)"

5
(5, 6)"

4 (5, 6)"

9
(10½, 10½)"

22
(26, 28)"

**Front**

13
(15½, 17½)"

10½ (11½, 13)"

19 (21, 21)"

**Sleeve**

16
(17, 18)"

**Cuff**

4"

8 (11, 11)"

18 (20, 22)"

4"    **Collar**

# Diagonal-Knit Pullover

*Summer* ♦ *Advanced*

## KNITTED MEASUREMENTS

SIZES: Small (Medium, Large)
FINISHED BUST: 36 (40, 44)"
LENGTH: 21 (22, 24)"

## MATERIALS

♦ 3 (3, 4) skeins of Light Stuff by Prism Yarns (mixed fiber content, 400 yds/6–7oz), Fog
♦ 2 size 5 circular knitting needles (24"), or size required to obtain gauge
♦ Size G crochet hook

## GAUGE

22 sts and 36 rows = 4" in pattern stitch

## PATTERN STITCH FOR GAUGE SWATCH

*(Multiple of 12 sts and 24 rows)*
CO 36 sts.
**Rows 1, 3, 5, 7, 9, 11 (WS):** (K6, P6) across
**Row 2 and all even-numbered rows:** K across.
**Rows 13, 15, 17, 19, 21, 23:** (P6, K6) across.
Rep these 24 rows.

## LEFT BACK BEGINNING TRIANGLE

FOLLOW CHART for your size. The chart shows whether a square is garter stitch or stockinette stitch with the RS facing you. Mark off the sections as you complete them. I have outlined the first 2 sections below so that you can see how the pattern works.

CO 7 sts.

**Row 1 (WS):** K6, P1.

**Row 2 and all even-numbered rows:** K1, M1, K across.

**Row 3:** K6, P2.

**Row 5:** K6, P3.

**Row 7:** K6, P4.

**Row 9:** K6, P5.

**Row 11:** K6, P6.

From this point, each section has 12 rows. At the end of the 12 rows, you should have 6 garter-stitch ridges in each garter-stitch section.

**Row 13:** CO 6 sts, K6, P6, K6, P1.

**Row 15:** K6, P6, K6, P2.

**Row 17:** K6, P6, K6, P3.

**Row 19:** K6, P6, K6, P4.

**Row 21:** K6, P6, K6, P5.

**Row 23:** (K6, P6) twice.

Cont in this manner, following chart and working extra sts into pattern on WS. End on row 59 for small, row 71 for medium, or row 83 for large and set aside with all sts on needle.

# RIGHT BACK BEGINNING TRIANGLE

FOLLOW CHART for your size. I have outlined the first 2 sections below.

CO 7 sts.

**Row 1 (WS):** P1, K6.

**Row 2 and all even-numbered rows without cast on:** K to 1 st from end, M1, K1.

**Row 3:** P2, K6.

**Row 5:** P3, K6

**Row 7:** P4, K6.

**Row 9:** P5, K6.

**Row 11:** P6, K6.

From this point, each section has 12 rows. At the end of the 12 rows, you should have 6 garter-stitch ridges in each garter-stitch section.

**Row 12:** CO 6 sts, K to 1 st from the end, M1, K1.

**Row 13:** P1, K6, P6, K6.

**Row 15:** P2, K6, P6, K6.

**Row 17:** P3, K6, P6, K6.

**Row 19:** P4, K6, P6, K6.

**Row 21:** P5, K6, P6, K6.

**Row 23:** (P6, K6) twice.

Cont in this manner, following chart and working extra sts into pattern on WS. End on row 59 for small, row 71 for medium, or row 83 for large and set aside with all sts on needle.

To join the 2 triangles, work across the right back triangle as follows: K1, M1, K to 1 st from end of right triangle, M1, K1, PM, working up left back triangle, K1, M1, K to 1 st from end of left back triangle, M1, K1. **Next row:** P1, (K6, P6) 4 (5, 6) times, K6, P14, (K6, P6) 4 (5, 6) times, K6, P1. **Next row and all RS rows:** K1, M1, K to 3 sts from marker, K2tog, K1, slip marker, K1, SSK, K to last st, M1, K1. **Next row:** P2 (K6, P6) 4 (5, 6) times, K6, P12, (K6, P6), 4 (5, 6) times, K6, P2. Cont in this manner, working inc at beg and end of RS rows and 2 decs at center. Center 4 sts remain in St st. Work inc and dec into pattern st on WS rows.

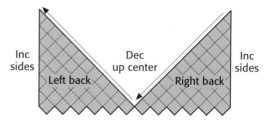

## *Armholes*

CONT WITH chart, working only the decreases at the center for the next 24 rows.

## *Back Shoulder and Neck Shaping*

**All RS rows:** SSK, cont to work 2 decreases in center, work to last 2 sts, K2tog. **All WS rows:** work dec into patt st. Work these last 2 rows until 6 sts remain, S1, K2tog, psso, SSSK. P2tog, finish off.

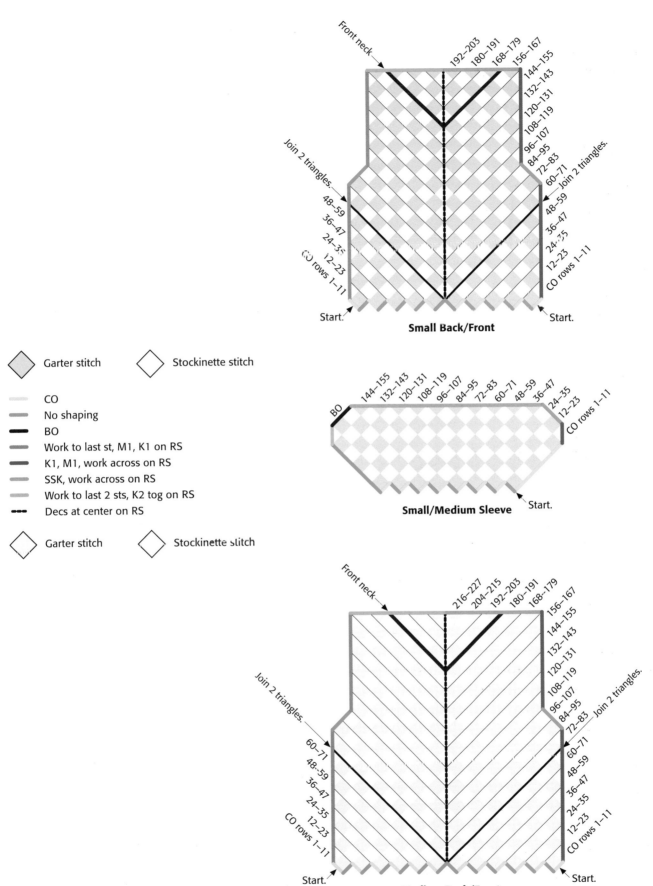

**Small Back/Front**

**Small/Medium Sleeve**

**Medium Back/Front**

Garter stitch    Stockinette stitch

CO
No shaping
BO
Work to last st, M1, K1 on RS
K1, M1, work across on RS
SSK, work across on RS
Work to last 2 sts, K2 tog on RS
Decs at center on RS

Garter stitch    Stockinette stitch

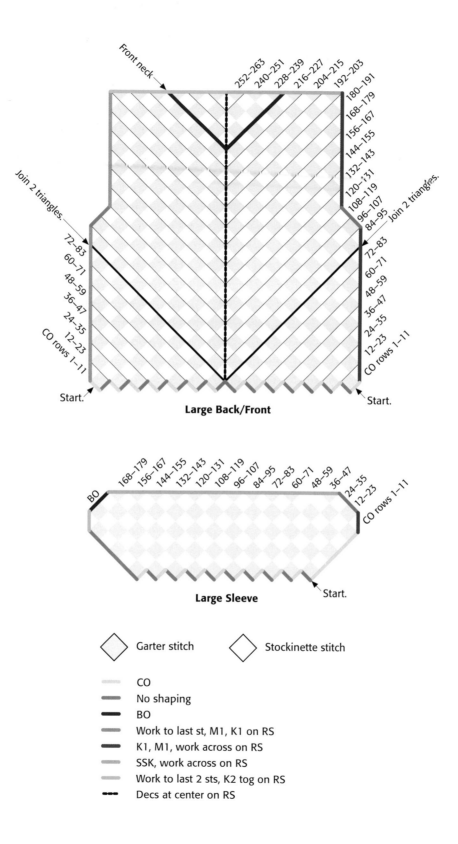

**Large Back/Front**

Front neck

252–263
240–251
228–239
216–227
204–215
192–203
180–191
168–179
156–167
144–155
132–143
120–131
108–119
96–107
84–95
72–83
60–71
48–59
36–47
24–35
12–23
CO rows 1–11

Join 2 triangles.

Start.

**Large Sleeve**

168–179
156–167
144–155
132–143
120–131
108–119
96–107
84–95
72–83
60–71
48–59
36–47
24–35
12–23
CO rows 1–11

BO

Start.

◇ Garter stitch          ◇ Stockinette stitch

CO
No shaping
BO
Work to last st, M1, K1 on RS
K1, M1, work across on RS
SSK, work across on RS
Work to last 2 sts, K2 tog on RS
‑‑‑ Decs at center on RS

## FRONT

WORK AS for back until 76 (76, 76) sts remain for V neck. BO all sts.

## SLEEVES (MAKE 2)

CO 31 (31, 31) sts. Work chart for your size.

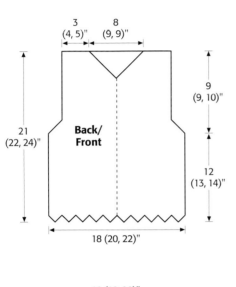

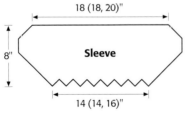

## FINISHING

Weave tog shoulder seams.

Starting at right shoulder seam, work a row of sc around the neck edge, skipping 2 sts at the center front V neck. Join with a sl st. Do not turn, work a row of reverse sc. Finish off.

Weave sleeve into armhole. Weave side seam and sleeve seam.

Lay flat, spray with water, and smooth. Do not remove until dry.

# Short Rows

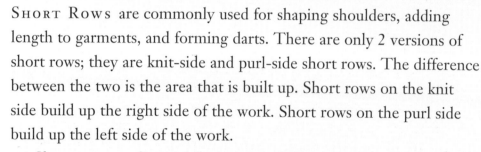

SHORT ROWS are commonly used for shaping shoulders, adding length to garments, and forming darts. There are only 2 versions of short rows; they are knit-side and purl-side short rows. The difference between the two is the area that is built up. Short rows on the knit side build up the right side of the work. Short rows on the purl side build up the left side of the work.

Short rows can be used for knitting different yarns and colors into your sweaters as well. Using short rows for color work will resemble intarsia, but it will be a bit easier. Short rows are also a good tool for knitting multicolored yarns to create diagonal lines that add more interest and texture to a garment. See Swim with the Fish Short-Rows Vest (page 104) and the border on the Short-Rows Border Cardigan with Black-and-White Tucks (page 110).

Short rows are not limited to stockinette stitch. They can also be worked in other pattern stitches like garter stitch or seed stitch as long as the placement of the short rows does not interfere with or show in the pattern.

Using short rows in knitting is one more intriguing method to make your knitting unique and different.

## KNIT-SIDE SHORT ROWS

Knit to the designated stitch, slip the next stitch on the left needle to the right needle as if to purl. Move the yarn between the needles toward you, move the stitch back to the left needle. Be sure the yarn is down and out of your way. Move the yarn through the needles toward the back of the work, turn and purl back across the stitches that were previously knit. The yarn will be wrapped around the stitch. This step is called "wrap and turn" (W and T). The yarn wrapped around the stitch looks like a purl bar on the right side. There will also be a gap between the stitches on the needle.

After all short rows are complete, you will need to knit one last row so that the yarn wrapped around the stitches will get knitted to the stitch on the needle above it. The wrap will then no longer be visible on the right side of the work.

To knit up the wraps, knit to the stitch that has the yarn wrapped around it. Insert the right knitting needle under the wrap on the right side and knit it together with the stitch it is wrapped around. This will force the extra yarn that was wrapped around the stitch to the back. This process is called knitting up the wraps.

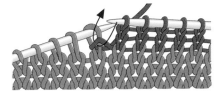

## PURL-SIDE SHORT ROWS

Purl to the designated stitch, slip the next stitch on the left needle to the right needle as if to purl. Move the yarn between the needles away from you, move the stitch back to the left needle. Move the yarn through the needles toward the front of the work, turn and knit back across the stitches that were previously purled. The yarn wrapped around the stitch will look like a purl bar on the right side. There will also be a gap between the stitches on the needle.

To purl up the wraps, purl to the stitch that has the yarn wrapped around it. Insert the right knitting needle under the wrap on the knit side of the work and purl it together with the stitch it is wrapped around. This is a bit awkward; try lifting the stitches off one at a time to force the extra yarn that was wrapped around the stitch to the back.

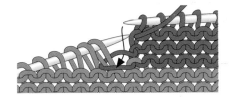

**Caution:** Never knit or purl past a wrap without "knitting (or purling) it up." It cannot be retrieved later. The only exception is when the wraps are used as a decorative element, as in the triangle border on the Short Rows Border Cardigan with Black-and-White Tucks. There are many times when you will knit or purl across a previously wrapped stitch to create the next short row. Be sure to knit or purl the wrap up as you go by it.

## SHORT ROWS FOR SHOULDER SHAPING

Most patterns call for bound-off stitches for sloping shoulder seams. It is very difficult to weave together such an edge without bulk. Try using short rows to create the slope, leaving all the stitches on the needle so you can join the shoulders with the 3-needle BO (see page 10). The short-rows method creates a smoother seam.

Use knit-side short rows to create the left front shoulder and the right back shoulder slope. Use purl-side short rows to create the right front shoulder and the left back shoulder slope.

A sloped shoulder needs to be higher at the neck edge than at the armhole edge. When you work the slope using bound-off stitches in sections, you start binding off at the armhole edges. When you use short rows, you will leave the number of stitches you were supposed to bind off behind, so to speak, by knitting or purling to the designated number, wrapping and turning, and working back. For example, for the right back or left front shoulder, if the pattern tells you to bind off 4 stitches at the armhole edge once, then 5 stitches 3 times, and finally the remaining 4 stitches, you would work the short rows as follows.

Knit across shoulder stitches, turn, purl across shoulder to last 4 sts, wrap and turn, knit back, (purl to 5 stitches from the previous wrap, wrap and turn, knit back) 3 times, there are 4 stitches remaining. Purl 1 more row, purling up wraps. Place stitches on holder.

For the left back or right front shoulder: Knit across to the last 4 stitches, wrap and turn, purl back, (knit to 5 stitches from the previous wrap, wrap and turn, purl back) 3 times, there are 4 stitches remaining. Knit 1 more row, knit up the wraps. You are now ready to work 3-needle BO to join the shoulders.

Putting in the short rows will "feel" like you are doing the opposite of what the stair-step BO told you to do.

## SHORT ROWS FOR COLOR WORK

I love using short rows for color work. It is easier than intarsia because only one color or section is worked at a time. There are also fewer ends to weave in, and most of them end up on the edges.

Each of the four garments in this section uses the short-row technique a little differently. In the first garment, Garter-Stitch Short-Rows Pullover, short rows add single stripes of color in garter stitch. In Swim with the Fish Short-Rows Vest, the short rows create entire sections, showing off the multicolored yarn. Short rows form the border triangles in the Short-Rows Border Cardigan with Black-and-White Tucks. In Short-Rows Color-Work Cardigan, short rows make large triangular sections that form the body and sleeves.

## SHORT ROWS IN CHARTS

To work charts with short rows, work to vertical line on chart, wrap and turn the next stitch, and knit or purl back as directed.

**Note:** When working short rows, *always* move the stitch from the left needle to the right needle first, move the yarn to the opposite side, place the stitch back on the left needle, move the yarn to opposite side, and turn. Use this abbreviated form to help you remember the wrap and turn: Move the stitch, yarn, stitch, yarn—in that order—and you won't go wrong.

# TUCK STITCH

I've added some "tucks" in 2 of the following projects to increase the interest and hide the slight stitch distortions that happen when you do a lot of short rows in one row. The tuck stitch is used to create a raised ridge of stitches. It can be worked in one or more colors, depending on the desired look.

## Basic Tuck Stitch

Work the required number of rows in the specified color as indicated in the pattern.* Turn the work to the wrong side, and with a small double-pointed needle, pick up about 6 to 8 of the purl bars of the same color you are using (1), ending at the same edge as the tip of the main knitting needle. Turn the work to the right side and knit together 1 stitch from each needle, folding the tuck in half (2). Cont from * across the row until all stitches are knit together and the tuck is finished; you will be 1 picked-up stitch short. Knit the last stitch on the needle by itself.

## Two-Color Tuck Stitch

Work the number of rows specified in the directions using the two-color tuck stitch. Work tuck as for basic tuck; be sure yarn floats are inside the tuck (1).

**Note:** If you have difficulty finding the purl bar to make the tuck because of the yarn floats across the wrong side, drop to the row below where it is easier to see.

## Bind Off in Tuck Stitch

Work as described above for basic tuck stitch, except when there are 2 stitches on the right needle, bind off loosely. Cont across the row, knitting the tuck together and binding off when there are 2 sts on the right needle. Continue across until all sts are bound off.

# Tuck and Roll Short-Rows Purse

## KNITTED MEASUREMENTS

8" wide x 7" high x 2½" deep

## MATERIALS

- Cotton Twist by Berroco (70% mercerized cotton and 30% rayon, 85yds/50g)
  - 2 skeins sunshine yellow 8317 (MC)
  - 2 skeins white 8301 (CC1)
  - 1 skein black 8390 (CC2)

- 2 size 6 circular needles (24"), or size required to obtain gauge
- 1 size 3 double-pointed needle
- Size G crochet hook
- ½ yd. fabric for lining
- ½ yd. Pellon Craft-Fuse
- Small bottle or bowl to shape handle
- 1 button, 1" diameter

NOTE: *If you choose yarns other than the ones specified, be sure they are colorfast so the accent colors do not bleed onto the main color when the purse is washed.*

## GAUGE

21 sts and 28 rows = 4" in St st on size 6 needles

## FRONT

WITH SIZE 6 needles and MC, CO 40 sts. Work St st for 34 rows. Dec 1 st at each end EOR 4 times. BO all sts. Trace front shape on piece of paper to use as pattern for the lining later.

## GUSSET

HOLD FRONT with RS facing. With CC1, start at BO row, going down left edge, PU 32 sts to bottom edge, 31 sts across bottom edge, 32 sts on opposite side—95 sts. **Work 2-color tuck: Row 1:** (P5 in CC1, P5 in CC2) to last 5 st, P5 in CC1. Work St st for 2 more rows in colors as set. Make tuck (see page 95). **Next row:** P across with CC1. Beg short-row shaping. K to 8 sts from end, W and T (see page 93), P back to 8 sts from end, W and T, K back to 12 sts from end, W and T, P back to 12 sts from end, W and T, K back across all sts, picking up wraps as you pass them. P back to end, picking up wraps as you pass them. Do not BO. Leave sts on needles and set aside. Cut yarn.

Measure length and width of gusset and make a paper pattern for lining.

## BACK

WITH THE second size 6 needles, work as for front and gusset. With WS together, work 3-needle BO, (see page 10) to join gusset pieces.

## FLAP

HOLD BACK with RS facing. With MC, PU 35 sts. Work St st for 2". Dec 1 st at each end EOR 4 times. BO 3 sts at beg of next 2 rows once. BO 5 sts at beg of next 2 rows once. BO rem sts.

**Tuck on edge of flap:** Hold flap with RS facing. With CC1, PU 55 sts, P 1 row. (K5 in CC2, K5 in CC1) around, end K5 in CC2. Work St st in colors as set for 3 more rows. K 1 row, P 1 row in CC1. Work tuck as for gusset except BO all sts at the same time.

## FINISHING

### Button Loop

CH 12 sts or the number of chs that will go around the button you have chosen. Turn, skip first ch, sc into each ch across. Finish off. Fold into a loop and sew to center of flap about ½" in from the tuck on the WS.

### Edging

WORK A row of sc across front edge of purse.

### Strap

WITH CC1, CO 7 sts, work St st for 18" or approximately 100 rows. BO. With CC2, PU 85 sts on long edge of strap. (P5 in CC2, P5 in CC1) across, end P5 in CC2. Work St st in colors as set for 3 more rows. Work tuck as for gusset, except BO all sts at the same time. Rep for other side of strap.

### Strap Lining

CUT A piece of fabric the width of the strap plus ¼" seam allowance on all sides. Cut iron-on interfacing to match without the ¼" seam allowance. Iron interfacing to back of lining. Hand stitch interfaced lining to WS of strap covering BO sts. Dampen the strap and wrap WS of wet strap against the bottle or bowl. I used a small fabric-softener bottle. Pin tog ends and allow to dry. After strap is dry, sew to top of gusset, easing to fit. Attach to tucks at edges of gusset. Weave in all ends.

See "Lining Purses" on page 124 for lining instructions. Sew on the button.

# Garter-Stitch Short-Rows Pullover

*Fall ♦ Beginner*

## KNITTED MEASUREMENTS

SIZES: Small (Medium, Large)
FINISHED BUST: 36 (40, 44)"
LENGTH: 21 (22½, 24)"

## MATERIALS

♦ Kid n Ewe by Bryspun (50% Kid Mohair, 50% Wool, 120yds/50g)
  · 8 (10, 12) skeins color 580 (MC)
  · 1 (1, 1) skein color 340 (CC1)
  · 1 (1, 1) skein color 510 (CC2)
  · 1 (1, 1) skein color 540 (CC3)
  · 1 (1, 1) skein color 740 (CC4)
♦ Sizes 5 and 7 circular needles (24"), or size required to obtain gauge

## GAUGE

18 sts and 24 rows = 4" in stockinette stitch on size 7 needles

NOTE: *This garment is knit from side seam to side seam; row gauge is very important, as it determines the size or width of the piece.*

## GARTER-STITCH SHORT ROWS

WHEN YOU come to a colored horizontal line on the chart, use the appropriate color and work a short row as follows. Do not count it as a row of the knitting on the chart.

♦ After a K row: With new color, P the appropriate number of sts as shown on chart, W and T, P back. P up the wrap with MC when you pass it on the next row (see page 93).

♦ After a P row: With new color, K the appropriate number of sts as shown on chart, W and T, K back. K up the wrap with the MC when you pass it on the next row.

## BACK

WITH SIZE 7 needles and MC, CO 54 (59, 64) sts. Beg chart at appropriate row number for your size, work in St st until you reach a colored line on chart. Work garter-stitch short rows as described above. When you reach the row where sts are added for armhole, use cable cast on (see page 7) to CO 41 (44, 45) sts. Cont with chart, work shoulder shaping: inc as shown for right shoulder, and dec for left shoulder. **For neck shaping:** BO sts as shown on chart for right half of neck. CO sts as shown for left neck. At left armhole, BO 41 (44, 45) sts. Finish chart. BO all sts.

## FRONT

WORK AS for back, using neck shaping for front on chart.

## SLEEVES (MAKE 2)

NOTE: *Sleeves are knit across instead of from wrist to armhole.*

With size 7 needles, CO 88 (92, 96) sts. Beg chart, work short rows on the knit side as indicated for your size. These short rows are for shaping. K up the wraps as you pass them. Work short-row color work as designated on chart. Work short rows at opposite end of chart. BO all sts.

### Sleeve Border

RS of sleeve facing, with size 5 needles and MC, PU 44 (54, 64) sts, turn. K 1 row in MC, K 2 rows in CC1, K 2 rows in CC2, K2 rows in CC3, K 2 rows in CC4. K 1 row in MC. **Picot BO:** *using cable cast on, CO 2 sts, BO 6 sts, move st on right needle back to left needle*. Rep from * to * across. Finish off.

## FINISHING

### Shoulder Seams

**Left front:** *RS facing, with CC2, PU 19 (24, 28) sts on left shoulder, K 1 row,* set aside. **Left back:** Rep from * to * with CC1. Hold with RS tog, work 3-needle BO, finish off. **Right front:** Rep as for left front with CC4. **Right back:** Rep as for left back with CC3.

### Neck Border

WITH SIZE 5 needles and MC, beg at right shoulder seam, PU 46 (50, 54) sts to left shoulder seam, 19 (21, 22) sts to beg of front neck shaping, 20 (24, 28) sts across center front, and 19 (21, 22) sts to right shoulder seam—104 (116, 126) sts. Do not join. Knit and BO as for sleeve border. Weave border seam together at right shoulder.

### Front and Back Bottom Border

WORK EACH piece separately. RS facing, with size 5 needles and MC, PU 85 (95, 105) sts on bottom edge of piece. Knit and BO as for sleeve border.

### Other Finishing

WEAVE SLEEVE into armhole, fitting top 1 (1½, 2)" of sleeve into bottom edge of armhole. Weave sleeve and side seams together.

Weave in all ends. Steam gently and lay flat to dry.

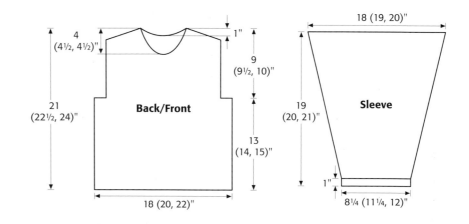

**Back**

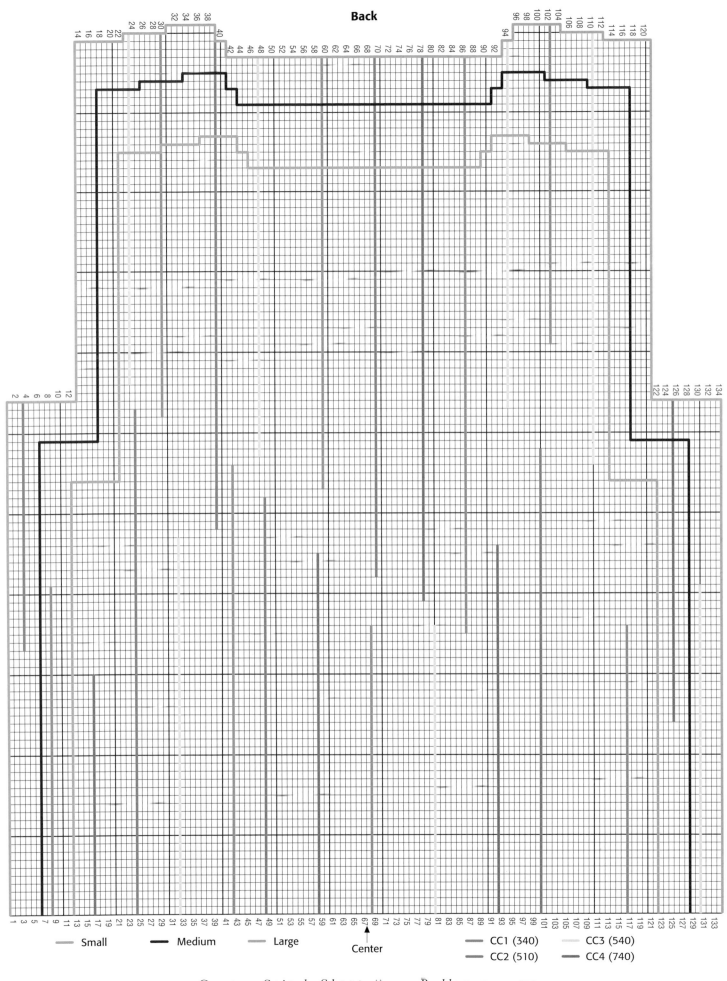

Small     Medium     Large       CC1 (340)    CC3 (540)

Center       CC2 (510)    CC4 (740)

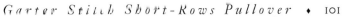

*Garter Stitch Short-Rows Pullover* ♦ 101

**Front**

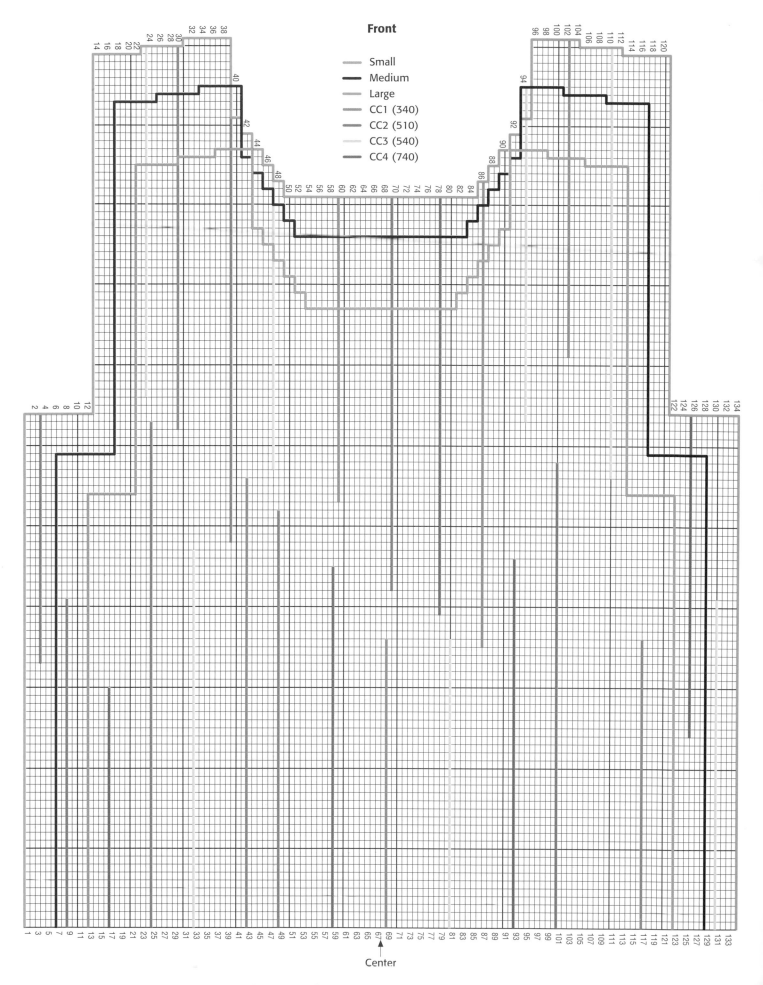

| | Small |
|---|---|
| | Medium |
| | Large |
| | CC1 (340) |
| | CC2 (510) |
| | CC3 (540) |
| | CC4 (740) |

Center

## Sleeve

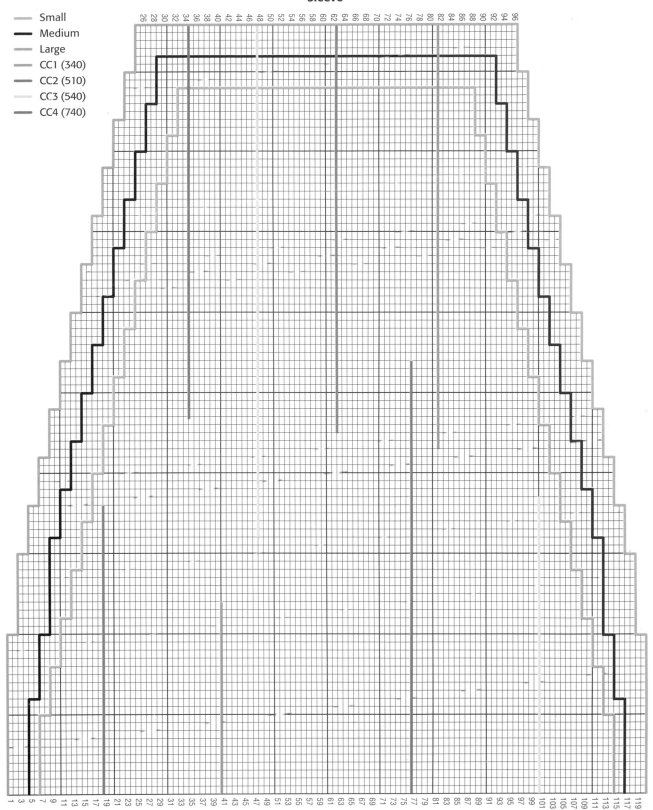

# Swim with the Fish Short-Rows Vest

*Summer* ◆ *Intermediate*

## KNITTED MEASUREMENTS

SIZES: Small (Medium, Large)
FINISHED BUST: 40 (43, 46)"
LENGTH: 21¾ (22¾, 23¾)"

## MATERIALS

◆ 8 (9, 10) skeins of Believe Cotton/Rayon by Classic Elite Yarns (77% cotton, 23% rayon, 93yds/50g) (MC)
◆ Provence by Classic Elite Yarns (100% Mercerized Cotton, 256 yds/125g)
  • 1 skein, color 2648 (CC1)
  • 1 skein, color 2681 (CC2)

◆ Sizes 6 and 7 circular needles (24"), or size required to obtain gauge
◆ Size 6 circular needles (29"), for front back and neck border and bottom band
◆ 15 fish buttons (7 used for embellishment), ¾" diameter

## GAUGE

20 sts and 28 rows = 4" in stockinette stitch on size 7 needles

NOTE: *This garment is worked from the right front around to the left front. Row gauge is very important as it determines the size. There are no side seams. The only seams to sew are the shoulder seams.*

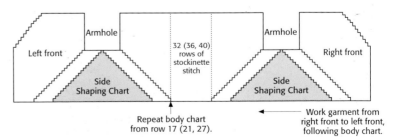

# RIGHT FRONT

WITH SIZE 7 needles and MC, CO 105 (110, 115) sts. K the first row of the body chart for your size. Beg short-row shaping for neck on next P row. At the same time on row 17 (21, 27), *beg short-row shaping for side edge. When short rows are completed, BO 44 (47, 51) sts for armhole, K up wraps as you cont across the row. Work 13 more rows in St st, ending with a P row. K 2 rows with CC1, K 2 rows with CC2. The last 4 rows are not shown on the chart.

# SIDE SHAPING

GO TO side shaping chart (page 109). With MC, K 1 row, beg short rows for your size on next P row. Don't forget to purl up wraps as you pass them. When short rows are completed, K 1 row and work other side of chart, starting on next P row. When chart is completed, P 1 row, purling up wraps. K 2 rows with CC2, K 2 rows with CC1. The last 4 rows are not shown on the chart. Return to body chart (page 108): Work 14 rows in St st, CO 44 (47, 51) sts for armhole at beg of next row. Beg short-row shaping for back on next K row, be sure to K up wraps as you pass them. Do not work neck shaping at end of chart until center left front.* Work 32

(36, 40) rows in St st. These rows are not shown on chart.

# LEFT BACK AND LEFT FRONT

WORK BODY chart again, starting at row 17 (21, 27); do not do short rows for right neck shaping. Follow from * to * in "Right Front" and "Side Shaping." Beg short rows for left front neck shaping on next P row 34 (38, 44) rows from armhole. When short rows are completed, work across entire row, purling up the wraps. BO all sts.

# FINISHING

## Seams

WEAVE TOG shoulder seams.

## Armhole Borders

WITH SIZE 6 needles, RS facing, and CC1, starting at midpoint of underarm, PU 12 sts on flat area of underarm, 42 (45, 49) sts to shoulder seam, 42 (45, 49) sts to flat area of underarm, PU 12 sts—108 (114, 122) sts. *K 1 row in CC1. K 2 rows in CC2. With CC1, work K1, P1 rib for 4 rows*. BO loosely.

## Bottom Border

RS OF left front facing, with size 6 needles and CC1, PU 24 (28, 34) sts to first set of garter-stitch ridges, 68 (76, 84) sts to next set of garter-stitch ridges, 57 (63, 68) across mid-back section to next set of garter-stitch ridges, 68 (76, 84) sts to next set of garter-stitch ridges, 24 (28, 34) sts to left front edge. Work from * to * of armhole border.

## Front Band and Neck Border

RS OF right front facing, with size 6 needles and CC1, PU 5 sts on bottom band, 55 (58, 61) sts to V neck, 35 (38, 41) sts to right shoulder seam, 42 (45, 48) sts across back neck, 35 (38, 41) sts to end of V-neck shaping, 55 (58, 61) sts to bottom border, 5 sts on border. Work border as follows: K 1 row in

CC1. K 2 rows in CC2. With CC1, work K1, P1 rib for 2 rows. Work buttonhole row: K3 (5, 7) sts, SSK, YO, (K6, SSK, YO) 7 times, finish row. Work 3 more rows of ribbing. BO loosely.

## Other Finishing

WEAVE IN all ends. Lay flat, moisten and pin to shape; do not remove until completely dry. Sew on buttons and embellish with leftover buttons on left front and right back shoulder.

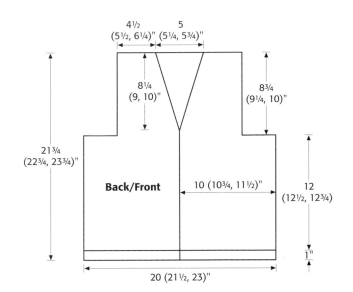

## Body Chart
### Section 2

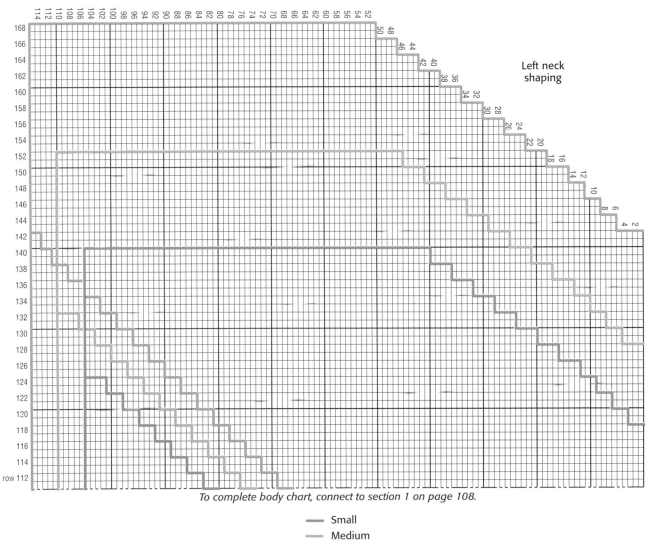

*To complete body chart, connect to section 1 on page 108.*

— Small
— Medium
— Large

# Body Chart
## Section 1
*To complete body chart, connect to section 2 on page 107.*

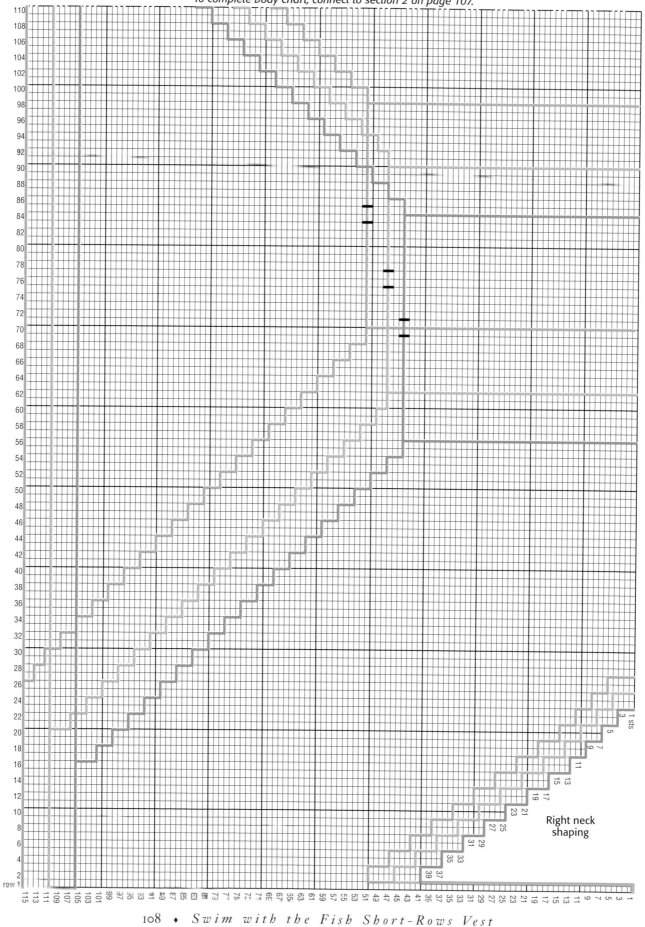

Right neck shaping

## Side Shaping Chart

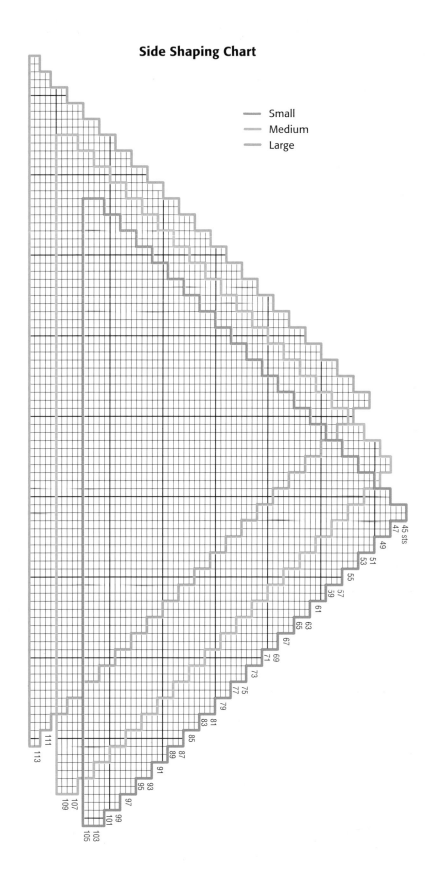

Small
Medium
Large

45 sts
47
49
51
53
55
57
39
61
63
65
67
69
71
73
75
77
79
81
83
85
87
89
91
93
95
97
99
101
103
105
107
109
111
113

# Short-Rows Border Cardigan with Black-and-White Tucks

*Spring* ♦ *Intermediate to Advanced*

## KNITTED MEASUREMENTS

SIZES: Small (Medium, Large)
FINISHED BUST: 36 (40, 44)"
LENGTH: 22 (23½, 24½)"

## MATERIALS

- Cotton Twist by Berroco (70% mercerized cotton, 30% rayon viscose, 85 yds/50g)
  - 14 (15, 16) skeins color 8311 (MC)
  - 2 (2, 2) skeins color 8347 (CC1)
  - 2 (2, 2) skeins color 8348 (CC2)
  - 1 (1, 1) skein color 8301 (CC3)
  - 1 (1, 1) skein color 8390 (CC4)
- Size 7 circular needles (24"), or size required to obtain gauge
- Size 6 circular needles (29")
- 2 size 6 double-pointed needles (for border)
- 1 size 2 double-pointed needle (to work tuck stitch)
- 4 stitch holders
- 6 buttons, ¾" diameter

NOTE: *If you choose to use yarns other than the ones specified, be sure they are colorfast so the MC and the contrasting colors do not bleed onto the white yarn used on the tuck.*

## GAUGE

20 sts and 28 rows in body = 4" in stockinette stitch on size 7 needles

NOTE: *The short rows used in the border of this cardigan are a bit different that the short rows used in the other sweaters in this section. The wraps are **not** knit up; they are left as part of the design.*

## RIGHT FRONT BAND AND BACK SHORT-ROWS BORDER

WITH SIZE 6 dpn and MC, CO 10 sts, *K 1 row. K9, W and T, K back. K8, W and T, K back. K7, W and T, K back. K6, W and T, K back. K5, W and T, K back. K4, W and T, K back. K3, W and T, K back. K2, W and T, K back. K1, W and T, K back. *Do not* K up wraps. Cut MC. Do not turn. Slide work to opposite end of dpn, away from the MC tail you just cut. Turn, with CC1: K1, W and T, K back. K2, W and T, K back. K3, W and T, K back. K4, W and T, K back. K5, W and T, K back. K6, W and T, K back. K7, W and T, K back. K8, W and T, K back. K9, W and T, K back.* Rep from * to * using MC as established and alternating CC1 and CC2. When there are 9 (10, 11) squares, BO. Piece should measure approximately 18 (20, 22)". If it is slightly larger, the size will dec slightly when you add the knitting to the bottom edge and add the tuck above the border.

## LEFT FRONT BAND AND BACK SHORT-ROWS BORDER

WORK AS for right front band, substituting MC where CC1 and CC2 were used, and substituting CC2 for MC for first rep of patt and CC1 for MC for second rep. Cont alternating colors as for right front band. When there are 9 (10, 11) squares, BO.

## TWO-COLOR TUCK ON RIGHT FRONT AND RIGHT BACK BORDER

**HOLD RIGHT front and back band with RS facing. With size 6 circ needles and CC3, PU 81 (90, 99) sts across top edge of band, starting at right front edge (this is the edge with CC1 and CC2; the MC should be at the bottom). **Row 1:** P with CC3. **Row 2:** (K3 with CC3, K3 with CC4) across, floating yarns loosely across the back. End with K3 in CC3. **Row 3:** (P3 in CC3, P3 in CC4), end P3 in CC3. **Row 4:** Rep row 2. **Row 5:** P with CC3. Make tuck with MC. (See page 95.) Change to size 7 needles, P back.**

## RIGHT FRONT

WORK ON first 36 (40, 45) sts only. With MC, K 1 row. Leave rem sts on an extra needle. Cont in MC, work in St st for 11½ (12½, 13)" from top of border. Beg armhole and neck shaping: at neck edge, dec 1 st every 3 (3, 3) rows 8 (16, 16) times, then every 4 (0, 4) rows 6 (0, 2) times, and at the same time work armhole shaping as follows: BO 6 (6, 8) sts at armhole edge, then dec 1 st EOR 6 (8, 9) times. When armhole measures 8 (8½, 9)", place rem 10 (10, 10) sts on a holder.

## TWO-COLOR TUCK ON LEFT BACK AND LEFT FRONT BORDER

WORK FROM ** to ** above in two-color tuck, starting at center back with RS of border facing PU sts.

## LEFT FRONT

WORKING ON last 36 (40, 45) sts only for left front (leave remainder of sts for back on another needle), rep "Right Front" directions. Reverse shaping.

## BACK

WEAVE BORDER seam at center back together, including tuck. Work across all of back sts from both needles—90 (100, 108) sts. Cont in St st until back measures same as front to armhole.

### Armhole Shaping

BO 6 (6, 8) sts at beg of next 2 rows. Dec 1 st each end EOR 6 (8, 9) times—66 (72, 74) sts. Cont in St st until armhole measures 2" less than armhole of front, end with a P row.

### Neck Shaping

WORK ACROSS first 14 sts, BO center 38 (44, 46) sts, cont across rem 14 sts. Use another ball of yarn to work both shoulders simultaneously, or work shoulders separately. Dec 1 st at neck edge EOR 4 times. When armhole measures the same as on front, join shoulders with 3-needle BO (see page 10).

## SLEEVE-CUFF BORDER AND SLEEVES (MAKE 2)

WORK AS in "Right Front Band and Back Short-Rows Border" for 4 (4, 5) squares. BO. Following directions for 2-color tuck for fronts, PU 36 (42, 42) sts across border, work tuck as described. Change to size 7 needles, P across in MC, inc 0 (0, 4) sts evenly spaced. Work St st, inc 1 st at each end every 4 (4, 4) rows 8 (8, 6) times, then inc 1 st at each end every 5 (5, 5) rows 12 (12, 17) times—76 (82, 92) sts.

### Cap Shaping

WHEN SLEEVE measures 16 (17, 17½)", BO 6 (6, 8) sts at beg of next 2 rows, dec 1 st at each end every row 5 (5, 4) times, then dec 1 st at each end EOR 16 (18, 19) times. BO rem 22 (24, 30) sts.

### Sleeve Edging

WITH RS facing, size 6 needles, and MC, PU 36 (42, 42) sts across bottom edge of sleeve band. K 2 rows, BO loosely. Finish off all ends.

## TWO-COLOR TUCK ON FRONT EDGE AND NECK

ON RIGHT front with RS facing, size 6 needles, and CC3, PU 132 (138, 144) sts to center back neck. P 1 row. With CC4, work 2 rows of 2-color tuck pattern as in "Two-Color Tuck on Right Front and Right Back Border." K 1 row with CC3. With MC, make tuck and BO. Rep for left front, starting at back neck. When tuck is completed, weave tog the tucks at the back neck.

# Finishing

## Left Front Border

WORK AS for "Right Front Band and Back Short-Rows Border" but make 10 (11, 11) squares. On outside edge of border, where MC predominates, hold with RS facing. With size 6 needles and MC, PU 102 (112, 116) sts. K 3 rows, BO loosely.

## Right Front Border

WORK AS for "Left Front Band and Back Short-Rows Border" but make 10 (11, 11) squares. PU sts on outside of border as for "Left Front," K 1 row.
**Buttonhole row:** K 3 (4, 6) sts, (YO, K2tog, K8) 5 times, YO, K2tog, finish row. K 1 row, BO loosely.

## Bottom Border

WITH RS facing, size 6 needles and MC, PU 13 sts across lower edge of right front band, 10 sts in each square across bottom edge, and 13 sts across lower edge of left front band. K 2 rows. BO loosely.

## Other Finishing

WEAVE BORDERS to BO sts of tuck on fronts to center back with contrast edge next to tuck, stretching slightly to make border fit curve of neck edge, and buttonholes end at V neck. Finish off all ends.

Weave sleeve cap into armhole. Weave tog sleeve and side seam. Lay flat, heavily mist with water, pin out to correct dimensions, and allow to dry. Sew on buttons.

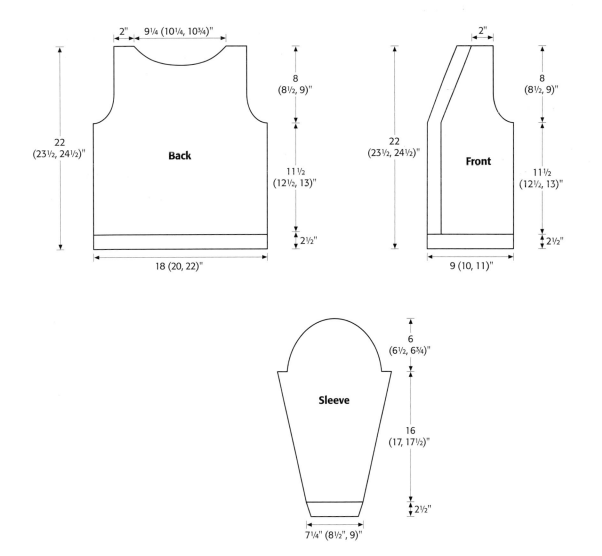

**Back**

2"

9¼ (10¼, 10¾)"

8
(8½, 9)"

22
(23½, 24½)"

11½
(12½, 13)"

2½"

18 (20, 22)"

**Front**

2"

8
(8½, 9)"

22
(23½, 24½)"

11½
(12½, 13)"

2½"

9 (10, 11)"

**Sleeve**

6
(6½, 6¾)"

16
(17, 17½)"

2½"

7¼" (8½", 9)"

# Short-Rows Color-Work Cardigan

## KNITTED MEASUREMENTS

SIZES: Small (Medium, Large)
FINISHED BUST: 40 (44, 48)"
LENGTH: 21½ (23, 24½)"

## MATERIALS

- Wild Stuff by Prism Yarns (mixed fiber content, 300yds/6–7oz)
  - 1½ (2, 2) skeins Tumbleweed (MC1)
  - 1½ (2, 2) skeins Nevada (MC2)
- Bon Bon by Prism Yarns (100% rayon, 94yds/57g)
  - 2 (2, 3) skeins color 106 (CC1)
  - 2 (2, 3) skeins Nevada (CC2)
  - 1 skein color 310 (CC3)
  - 1 skein color 314 (CC4)

- Sizes 5 and 7 circular needles* (24"), or size required to obtain gauge.
- Size 3 double-pointed needles (to work tuck stitch)
- 7 buttons, 1" diameter
- 4 stitch holders

*You must use size 7 circular needles because you will not always be starting a new yarn where you finished with the last yarn; you will slide the work down to the opposite end of the needle and start at the opposite end.

## GAUGE

18 sts and 24 rows = 4" in stockinette st with MC on size 7 needles

NOTE: *Row gauge is very important in this pattern.*

**Notes on reading the charts:** The charts for the front and back have "stair steps" drawn in black that show where the short rows are to be worked (see pages 121–122). Work to the st at the black line, W and T for a short row (see page 93). Cont in this manner for as many "steps" as are given on the chart. K or P back, making all the wraps, and then proceed to make the tuck as designated in the directions. The short-row sections are not complete until the wraps are knitted or purled up. Be sure to do this before you start the tucks. A tuck will be worked when all of the short rows are completed for each section as well as in the middle of a section where the horizontal lines are in the chart.

The "stair steps" for the sleeves are given in colors to designate size and shaping (see page 123). Work them the same as the color-work short rows: start with secotion A and short rows for shaping. Work appropriate tuck as given in the directions; then proceed to sections B and C where there is a short-row-color-work section. To finish off, the short rows at the end of section D are for shaping again.

All basic tucks are worked over 4 rows. All two-color tucks are worked over 3 rows, worked as K5 in one color, K5 in second color. Maintain colors for 3 rows.

# BACK

WITH SIZE 5 needles and CC1, CO 90 (100, 110) sts. K 4 rows. Change to size 7 needles, beg chart.

## Section 1

WITH MC2, beg chart. When the first set of short rows is completed, work a basic tuck with CC1 (see page 95).

## Section 2

HOLD BACK with WS facing. With MC1, work chart. When you have completed the first set of short rows for section 2, work a 2-color tuck with CC3 and CC4. This is the horizontal line through section 2 on the chart. Finish section 2 with MC1. When short rows are completed, work a basic tuck with CC2.

## Section 3

HOLD BACK with RS facing. With MC2, work chart. When you have completed the first set of short rows for section 3, work a basic tuck with CC1. This is the horizontal line in section 3 on the chart. Note the right armhole shaping takes place in section 3. Finish section 3 with MC2. Work a basic tuck with CC2.

## Section 4

HOLD BACK with WS facing. With MC1, work chart. When you have completed the first set of short rows for section 4, work a 2-color tuck with CC3 and CC4. This is the horizontal line through section 4 on the chart. Note left armhole shaping takes place on section 4. Finish section 4 with MC1. Work a basic tuck using CC1.

## Section 5

Hold back with RS facing. With MC2, work chart and neck shaping. When you have completed the first set of short rows for section 5, work a basic tuck with CC2. Finish section 5 with MC2. Work a basic tuck with CC1 over sts that were just short rowed on chart. This tuck will not go across the whole row due to neck shaping. Work rem rows of section 6. This completes the right shoulder. Place sts on a holder.

## Section 6

Hold back with RS facing. Rejoin MC at neck edge and work chart and neck shaping, including tucks. This completes the left shoulder. Place sts on a holder.

## FRONTS

WITH SIZE 5 needles and CC1, CO 45 (50, 55) sts, K 4 rows. Change to size 7 needles, follow chart as given for back, but work only the appropriate half.

## SLEEVES (MAKE 2)

NOTE: *The sleeves are knit across instead of up and down.*

WITH SIZE 7 needles and MC1, CO 86 (92, 96) sts. For small, work rows 1 through 36; for medium, work rows 1 through 40; for large, work rows 1 through 42, with short-row shaping as given in chart.

NOTE: *These short rows are for shaping, not for color work.*

Work a basic tuck with CC2. Hold with RS of section B facing. With MC2, start with row A and work rows A thru P2 for all sizes, working short rows as given for color work. Work a basic tuck st with CC1. Work section C, starting on the right side with MC1. Work a 2-color tuck with CC3 and CC4. Finish section D with MC2. For small, work rows 49 through 84; for medium, work rows 45 through 84; for large, work rows 43 through 84. Work short rows for shaping. BO.

### Sleeve Border

WITH SIZE 5 needles and CC1, PU 40 (44, 48) sts, K 5 rows. Change to CC2 and work 3-st I-cord BO (see page 9) until all sts of sleeve are used. BO rem 3 sts.

## FINISHING

### Seams

WEAVE TOG shoulder seams. Weave sleeves into sleeve openings. Weave sleeve seam together, grafting I cord at bottom band. Weave side seams together.

### Neck Band

WITH SIZE 5 needles and CC1, PU 80 (84, 88) sts around neck edge. K 5 rows. Change to CC2 and work 3-st I-cord BO. Do not BO last 3 sts; place on a holder.

### Front Bands

**Left side:** With size 5 needles and CC1, PU 90 (94, 98) sts along left front edge. K 5 rows. Change to CC2, CO 3 sts, and work 3-st I-cord BO. Graft together CO sts with the neck-edge I cord. Place rem 3 sts on a holder.

**Right side:** With size 5 needles and CC1, PU 90 (94, 98) sts along right front edge. K 3 rows. Work 7 buttonholes evenly spaced on next row: K2 (4, 3) sts, BO next 3 sts. [K11 (11, 12) sts, BO next 3 sts] 6 times, K2 (4, 3) sts. K next row, CO 3 sts over BO sts of previous row. K 1 row. Change to CC2 and work 3-st I-cord BO as for left front. Graft to neck-edge I cord.

### Bottom I Cord

WITH WS facing, size 5 needles, and CC1, PU every st around bottom edge. Turn, CO 3 sts, work 3-st I-cord BO across bottom. Do not BO. Graft both ends to front-band I cords.

### Other Finishing

STEAM GENTLY after weaving in all ends. Be careful not to flatten tucks. Sew on buttons.

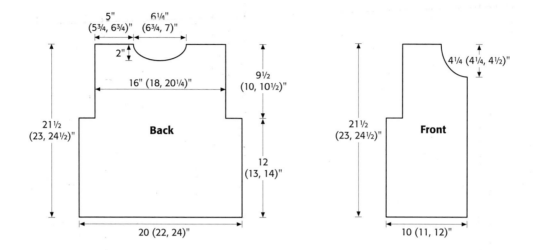

5"
(5¾, 6¾)"    6¼"
              (6¾, 7)"

2"

16" (18, 20¼)"

9½
(10, 10½)"

**Back**

21½
(23, 24½)"

12
(13, 14)"

20 (22, 24)"

4¼ (4¼, 4½)"

21½
(23, 24½)"

**Front**

10 (11, 12)"

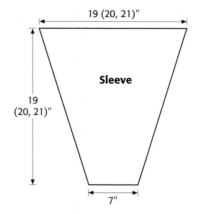

19 (20, 21)"

**Sleeve**

19
(20, 21)"

7"

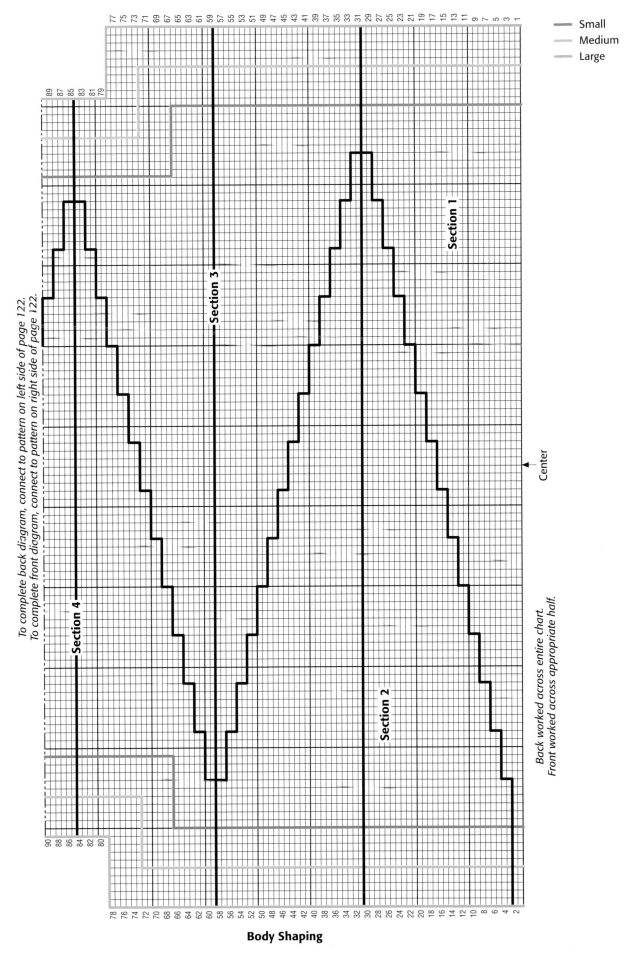

Small
Medium
Large

89 87 85 83 81 79

77 75 73 71 69 67 65 63 61 59 57 55 53 51 49 47 45 43 41 39 37 35 33 31 29 27 25 23 21 19 17 15 13 11 9 7 5 3 1

**Section 1**

**Section 3**

*To complete back diagram, connect to pattern on left side of page 122.*
*To complete front diagram, connect to pattern on right side of page 122.*

**Section 4**

Center

*Back worked across entire chart.*
*Front worked across appropriate half.*

**Section 2**

90 88 86 84 82 80

78 76 74 72 70 68 66 64 62 60 58 56 54 52 50 48 46 44 42 40 38 36 34 32 30 28 26 24 22 20 18 16 14 12 10 8 6 4 2

**Body Shaping**

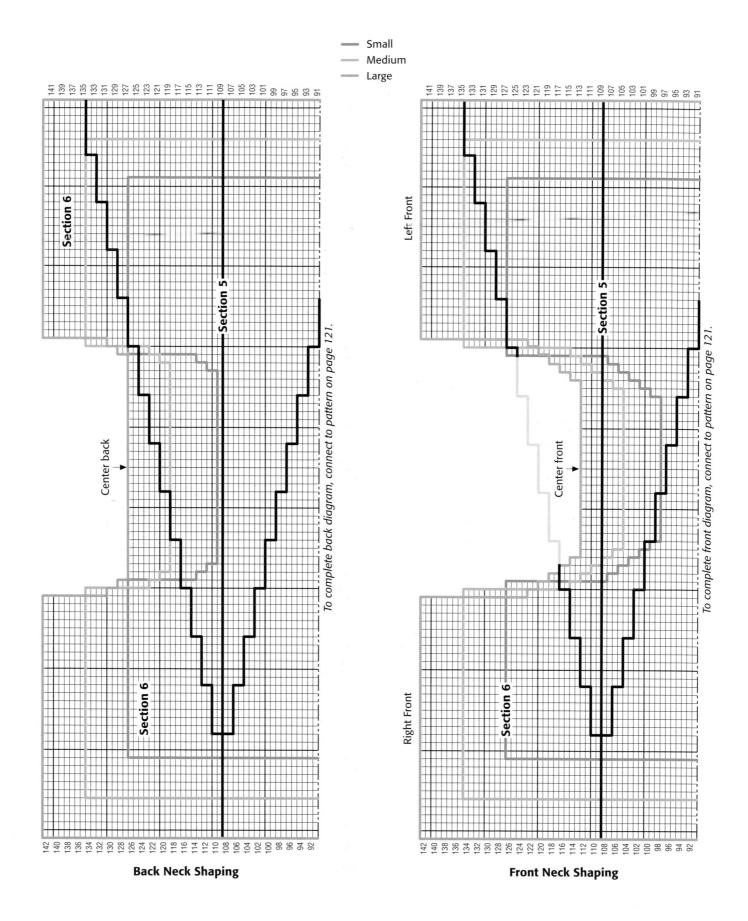

**Back Neck Shaping**

**Front Neck Shaping**

Small
Medium
Large

Section 6

Section 5

Center back

*To complete back diagram, connect to pattern on page 121.*

Left Front

Section 5

Center front

Right Front

Section 6

*To complete front diagram, connect to pattern on page 121.*

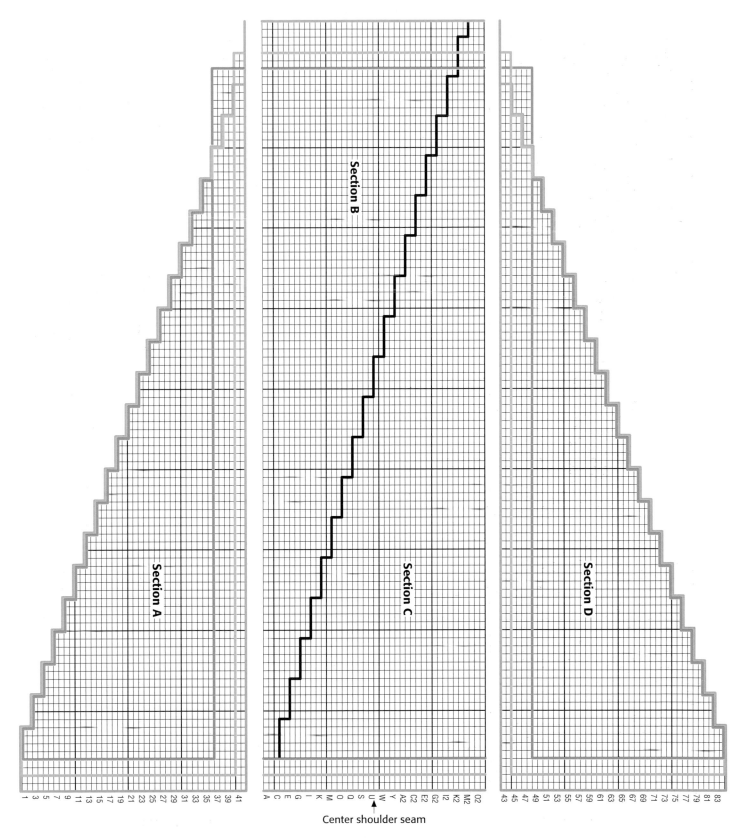

Center shoulder seam

**Sleeve**

# Lining Purses

PURSES WILL WEAR better and hold their shape longer if they are lined. To add body to purse lining, iron a craft-weight fusible web such as Pellon Craft-Fuse to the lining.

1. After knitting each piece for a purse, use the knitted shape to trace a pattern for the lining on a piece of paper. Add a ¼" seam allowance to the paper pattern.

2. Use the paper pattern pieces to cut the lining pieces.

3. Use the paper pattern pieces to cut pieces of Pellon Craft-Fuse for each purse as indicated below; remove the ¼" seam allowance from each piece.

   ♦ Diagonal-Knit Purse (page 65): 2 fronts, 2 backs, 2 gussets
   ♦ Pinwheel Purse (page 39): 2 fronts, 2 backs, 2 gussets
   ♦ Tuck and Roll Short-Rows Purse (page 96): 1 front, 1 back, 1 gusset

The Summer Slip-Stitch Tote Bag requires additional material to make it sturdier. Use the pattern pieces to cut the following pieces:

   ♦ From Heat 'n Bond Lite Iron-on Adhesive, cut 1 front, 1 back, 1 bottom, 2 pockets.
   ♦ From Pellon Craft-Fuse, cut 3 fronts, 3 backs, 3 bottoms, 2 pockets.
   ♦ From Pellon Thermolam, cut 1 front, 1 back, 1 bottom.

4. Follow manufacturer's directions to iron the Craft-Fuse to the lining. When using multiple layers of fusible web, iron over the previous layer. For the Summer Slip-Stitch Tote, iron the Heat 'n Bond Lite to the lining pieces first. Then remove the paper and iron the Thermolam to the fusible web. Then iron 3 pieces of Craft-Fuse to the Thermolam.

5. Sew together the lining pieces with a ¼" seam allowance. If your presser foot can't handle the bulk from the interfacings, try using a zipper foot to sew the seams. Clip the corners. Insert the lining into the purse to make sure it fits properly; adjust as necessary. Remove from purse. Fold the top of the lining ¼" toward the wrong side and press. Hand stitch the lining to the upper edge of the purse.

6. To make an inside zipper pocket for the Summer Slip-Stitch Tote Bag, cut the following pieces from the lining fabric:

   ♦ 2 pieces, 3" x 8"
   ♦ 2 pieces, 7" x 8"

With wrong sides facing, sew together the 7" x 8" pieces with a ¼" seam allowance, leaving an opening at the bottom. Repeat with the smaller pieces. Turn the pieces right sides out and press the seams. Hand sew the openings closed. Sew the narrower piece to the top of the zipper and the larger piece to the bottom of the zipper. Fold the ends of the zipper to the wrong side.

7. Machine sew the pocket to right side of the purse lining, ⅛" from edge of pocket, before sewing the lining to the purse.

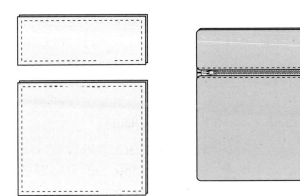

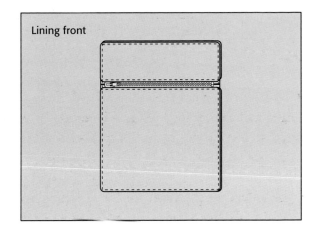

# Resources

My thanks to all of the following yarn and button companies for graciously supplying the materials needed for this book. For a list of stores in your area that carry the yarns and buttons mentioned in this book, write to the following companies.

## Yarns

Berroco, Inc.
PO Box 367
Uxbridge, MA 01569-0367

Brown Sheep Yarns
100662 CR 16
Mitchell, NE 69357

Bryson Distributing
4065 West 11th Avenue #39
Eugene, OR 97402

Canaan Mohair
430 du Gold Road
Hammond, ONT R0A2A0
Canada

Cascade Yarns
PO Box 58168
Tukwila, WA 98138-1168

Classic Elite Yarns
300A Jackson Street
Lowell, MA 01852

The Great Adirondack
Yarn Co.
950 County Highway 126
Amsterdam, NY 12010

Knit One, Crochet Two
2220 Eastman Avenue #105
Ventura, CA 93003-7794

Mountain Colors Yarns
PO Box 156
Corvallis, MT 59828

Muench Yarns and Buttons
285 Bel Marin Keys
Novato, CA 94949-5724

Prism Yarns
2595 30th Avenue N
St. Petersburg, FL 33713-2925

Tahki-Stacy Charles
Collection
1059 Manhattan Avenue
Brooklyn, NY 11222

Trendsetter Yarns
16742 Stagg Street, Suite 104
Van Nuys, CA 91406-1641

Rowan Yarns
Westminister Fibers, Inc.
5 Northern Boulevard #3
Amherst, NH 03031-2230

## Buttons

Blue Moon Button Art
406 Mission Street, Suite E
Santa Cruz, CA 95060
www.bluemoonbuttons.com

JHB International, Inc
1955 S. Quince Street
Denver, CO 80231

Knitropolis
343 Redondo Avenue
Long Beach, CA 90814